Surveys in Business and Economics 1

Marketing and Human Resources across Cultures

SURVEYS IN BUSINESS AND ECONOMICS

Series Editor

Wafik W.H. Kelliny

The goal of **SURVEYS IN BUSINESS AND ECONOMICS** is to address important topics meeting the needs of the growing number of business and economics scholars and professionals. Purposefully following a sequence from general principals to specific techniques, implementation strategies, and dissemination, the series volumes each examines interrelated aspects of business and economics. This comes in two forms, either a volume comprising a collection of edited papers by different authors, or a volume examining a particular aspect of business and economics research theme.

Volumes in the series:
1. **Surveys in Business and Economics 1:**
   Marketing and Human Resources across Cultures,
   By Wafik W.H. Kelliny
2. **Surveys in Business and Economics 2:**
   Perceptions of Organisations, Trainers and Employees
   of the Labour Market Needs
   By Wafik W.H. Kelliny and Salim Al Rizeiqi
3. **Surveys in Business and Economics 3:**
   Banking Business Environment and Staff Performance
   By Wafik W.H. Kelliny and Khalifa S. Al Said

Contributors may contact
the Series Editor:
kelliny@hotmail.com

Wafik W.H. Kelliny

Surveys in Business and Economics 1

Marketing and Human Resources across Cultures

First Published 2010
Series Editor: Wafik W.H. Kelliny
Charleston, SC
United States of America

British Library Cataloguing in Publication Data
Surveys in Business and Economics 1
- (Marketing and Human Resources across Cultures)
Business Studies – Global Marketing and Human Resources
I. Title   II. Series

ISBN   9781450587655

Library of Congress Cataloguing in Publication Data
Surveys in Business and Economics 1
- (Marketing and Human Resources across Cultures))
Business Studies – Global Marketing and Human Resources
Bibliography: p.
Includes indexes.
Business Studies – Surveys. I. Title   II. Series

To the memory of the dear ones,

Wadie H. Kelliny (1920 - 1978)

and Rose-Jameela S. Kamel (1928 -2009)

TABLE OF CONTENTS

ACKNOWLEDGEMENTS

I gratefully acknowledge the encouragement and support from many individuals and their organisations. Among those I would particularly express my gratitude to general managers, human resources and marketing managers and staff of global companies and suppliers who provided me with their valuable information, comments and insights.

Special thanks also go to personnel and organisations in Switzerland: Chambre Vaudoise du Commerce et de l'Industrie, Nestlé's Angus Freathy, Nestlé, Assistant Vice-President, Corporate HR-Training and Learning and Martinez, Director of HR Training and Learning, Sylvie Courvoisier, HR Director, Tetra Pak Export, and Jean Isler, Mandataire Commercial and Chef de Succursale, Siemens.

Thanks go to the Higher College of Technology students for collecting valuable data from the different areas of Muscat and other regions as well as the Ministry of Manpower, Oman, for providing me with valuable and informative data.

The enthusiastic feedback received from David Harness, Susan Miller, Laura Strang and my children Marc and Clara who have read parts of this work has been invaluable to me.

Last but not least, Sultan Qaboos University, and the University of Lausanne and the University of Geneva, Switzerland, for their unconditional professional support.

INTRODUCTION

The purpose of this volume is to identify the impact of cultural diversity on global companies' corporate behaviour, management, marketing strategies and human resources management. Accordingly, the review of literature examined the effects of cultural diversity on organisational culture and global management strategies, with particular reference to person environment-fit and market orientation in a multinational and multicultural context. In so doing, the study questions focused on customers' needs, wants and satisfaction and their perceptions of marketing strategies as well as employees' satisfaction, attitude, commitment, performance. This is in addition to the impact on marketing performance and innovation.

The effects of globalisation and the differences and similarities in the practices of marketing strategies and HRM in global businesses were also reviewed. Factors influencing marketing strategies and perceptions by firms, clients and staff were empirically examined. Accordingly, two global retailers in Oman were selected as the focus of the study. Global and local competitors were also referred to.

The study used the triangulation of research tools, data and sources using quantitative and qualitative test instruments to test the study's null hypotheses. The test instruments included questionnaires, semi-structured interviews, observations, documents and other sources of data. The main study sample comprised: 833 randomly selected customers from different areas and regions; 21 general managers from the two global retailers Carrefour and LuLu in Oman; 113 of their employees, and 10 managers of their suppliers of global products: Nestlé, Unilever, Sony, Canon, HP and IBM. This is in addition to managerial staff of several global companies and the Chamber of Commerce, Canton Vaud, in Switzerland

The study concluded that the success of managerial practices, marketing strategies, HRM and organisational design are dependent on an appropriate fit between the assumptions, values and beliefs inherent in the managerial practices in question and the culturally based assumptions, values and beliefs held by those who are being managed in global and multinational organisations and contexts.

1 The 'Fit' Concept in a Multinational Context and People's Success

I. Introduction: Success Depends on People

> "Nestlé is about people building brands. Throughout the Nestlé Group, we have exceptional people devoting their energy and skills to this task. Each year, we see many people joining our company and having the opportunity to broaden their expertise and experience by working on our brands. They also absorb our corporate culture, a unique mix of value orientation, internationality and commitment."
>
> Peter Brabeck-Lethmathe, CEO, quoted in Nestlé (2000, p. 3)

Indeed, it is a challenge for individual professionals and managers as well as global companies or institutions employing expatriates of different ethnic backgrounds, in addition to the national or local employees, to find the right proportion the right mix to fit between:

a. Organisational structure and contingency variables, i.e., in environmental adjustment or 'fit' of leaders, personnel and organisations to the environment within which they work.

b. Individual and organisational patterns of behaviour and value systems (Alder, 2002).

c. These organisational features or components and local, ethnic groups' and subgroups' cultures (Usunier, 1996).

This is usually a far-reaching challenge with long-term implications, which influence the success and prosperity of organisations or even host countries. This will also influence the corporate business strategy in a dynamic business environment, Burnes, (2000).

II. Cultural Diversity and the Dynamic Business Environment

Vérité en deça des Pyrénées, erreur au-delà.

"There are truths on this side of the Pyrénées [boarder mountains between France and Spain] which are falsehoods on the other. "

Blaise Pascal

Globalisation and Socio-cultural System

Due to globalisation, the effect of giant firms on local businesses and the extended effect of the turbulent dynamic world markets, we are now virtually functioning in a global village, is incredible. Accordingly, corporate world has become more and more internationally integrated. This has resulted in reshaping the face of organisational activities. Managers have also become aware of the complexity of various socio-cultural systems which have their impact on management (Drucker, 1954 and 1967). The ability to develop an intercultural competence in order to communicate/ interact and negotiate/manage in different settings effectively has to be realised by local and global companies, organisations and even academic institutions which employ staff of different backgrounds or have branches located overseas (Barlett and Goshal, 1989, 2000). Accordingly, the concept of culture has influenced the organisational theory and has become its core determining factor to obtain 'fit' in organisational settings (Alder, 1984; Usunier, 1996). This takes place through the environmental contingency factor, the 'national/social culture', as a kind of internal value system of the organisational structure (Lee, 2003).

Culture, however, has been a far reaching concept for the human brain or management to completely grasp. Accordingly, the following questions were raised:

"Will anyone ever again be able to write, with confidence, a book that assumes the significance of one culture only; will anyone ever again be able to stand upright in one nationality? Well, I spent a great deal of my life worrying about these things."

Drabble (1980), cited in Kelliny (1994, p.11)

Level of Analysis

Kroeber and Kulckhohn (1952, p. 357) described the complexity of the cultural concepts as comprising:

> "... patterns, explicit and implicit, of and for behavior acquired and transmitted by symbols constituting the distinguished achievements of human groups, including their embodiment in artifacts; the essential core of culture consists of traditional (i.e., historically derived and selected) ideas and especially their attached values; culture systems may, on the one hand, be considered as products of action, on the other hand, as conditioning elements for further action."

Hofstede's (1980, p. 25) widely accepted scientific definition of culture describing it as "... the collective programming of the human mind that distinguishes the members of one human group from those of another." Briefly, human behaviour of the firm's multi-culture staff, managers, customers or consumers has to be analysed in its socio-cultural context, if it is to be rightly understood and appreciated. Moreover, "Organisations not only operate within a socio-cultural context, but are being culture-bearing entities or cultural organisational behaviour. Nestlé, Unilever and other global organisations provide real-life examples in terms of management, marketing and HRD. For example, a primary objective of Nestlé organisational structure is standardised all over the world to ensure that the employees adjust to the company's structure, taking into accounts the incorporation of national cultures" (Freathy, 2006, p.7). This policy needs to be validated by further research in the areas of incorporation of local or national culture in theory building in managing global companies, as it has become more salient for researchers, e.g., Alder, 1983a, 1983b, 2002; Barrett and Bass, 1976; Boyacigiller and Adler, 1991; Hofstede, 1983; Shenkar and Von Glinow, 1994. In doing so, many issues have to be examined including:

a. Levels of cultural analysis (Antonakis et al., 2003)
b. The choice of relevant cultural dimensions (Hofstede, 1980; Robert et al., 2000; Smith et al., 1996; Tayeb, 2001)
c. The role of culture in the theoretical framework. In other words, is the direct influence or the moderating effect of culture to be examined or both? (Lincoln et al., 1981; Lincoln et al., 1986; Lincoln and Kalleberg, 1990).

According to Antonakis et al. (2004), organisations are inherently multileveled and may operate at one or more levels, as it the case of some global retailers, e.g. Carrefour and LuLu Hypermarkets in Oman, which are examined in this study. This also highlights the necessity to specify the level of analysis at which phenomena operate, as we cannot assume homogeneity of variations of units embedded in a higher order of a level factor.

Choice of Cultural Dimensions: A Case Study

Despite the popularity of Hofstede's model as well as the cultural dimensions suggested by other specialists, some scholars have been critical of the cultural dimensions in cross-cultural management research. For example, Tayeb (2001) urges scholars to avoid the dimensionalisation of local/national cultures indicating that culture is an elastic and woolly variable. This is because it is difficult to observe, identify and measure all its surface/visible and deep/hidden facets. This is a major factor for these personnel to fail to 'fit' in these categorisation and cultural dimensions. In other words, by putting culture into neat, sometimes unconnected little boxes, scholars, researchers and practitioners may lose sight of the entire situation.

Therefore, dimensionalisation should not be considered the only appropriate method to study cultures, as it still has its rationale as an operational/pragmatic method in making cross-cultural comparisons. Accordingly, the selection of cultural dimensions may vary from one study to the other, including their 'relevance' to the research topic and their 'robustness'. As Bhagat et al. (1990) indicated that the focus should be on the variations that are most relevant to a specific class of behaviours in a particular situation, ignoring some of the other subtle or less important variations.

'Robustness' of the crucial dimension is an important variable to ensure not only the pertinence and relevance of that dimension in management research, but also allowing comparisons across cultures. The emerging dimensions may include power distance, individualism, collectivism, uncertainty, avoidance, egalitarian commitment, integration, religion and Confucian work dynamics

(Buchanan and Huczynski, 2004; Harrison et al., 2000; Hofstede, 1980; Lee and Calvez, 2004; Robert et al., 2000).

Work-Related Value Differences

A. Power Distance (PD)

Table 1.1: Hofstede's Work Related Value

Category	Power Distance	Individualism vs. Collectivism	Uncertainty Avoidance	Masculinity vs. Femininity
Highest Score	104 (Malaysia)	91 (US)	92 (Japan)	95 (Japan)
Arab Countries	80	38	68	53
India	77	48	40	56
Lowest Score	18 (Denmark)	17 (Taiwan)	8 (Singapore)	5 (Sweden)

Work-related value differences as well as the organisational culture naturally influence the management style of the organisation and the aligning of the corporate objectives and the staff loyalty and commitment (Drucker, 1954 and 1967). On the other hand, leaders and managers have to take into account the environmental factors as even their discrete impact can jeopardise the performance of the firm.   Therefore, Hofstede's research findings (1980) are usually the most often quoted in the global management literature as a large study sample, 116,000 IBM employees worldwide was involved. His study questions were related to preferences in management styles, work values and information related to national origin.   Hofstede found the national cultures differed according to four main distinctions: Power distance (PD), individualism versus collectivism (I/C), uncertainty avoidance (UA), and masculinity versus femininity (M/F). Table 1 highlights relevant nationality/ethnic group in relation to their position in the cultural dimension to shed some light on our case studies either in the Sultanate of Oman and other countries through the following discussion of Hofstede's cultural dimensions.

Table 1.1 shows that high power distance societies will accept 'hierarchical' control and respect/submit to authority, i.e. Malaysia (104) while the other extreme is Denmark (18). According to the grouping of Hofstede's work-related differences' classification, Arab (80) and Indian (77) people are less likely to challenge authority or "contrast managerial and social science perspectives on organisational structure" (Buchanan and Huczynski, 2004, p. 669). But one may argue that individual's behaviour may also vary depending on the business environment including his/her job security, particularly in the Gulf countries.

B. Individualism versus. Collectivism

Individualism refers to a culture in which individuals look after their own immediate interests. This is true, particularly in western cultures and the US (91), in Arab societies (38) and India (48), but individuals and work-related conditions may result in different types of behaviour, i.e., being expatriates living away from their original social context can strengthen the level of individualism, in spite of being from a collectivism oriented culture. For example, Indian expatriates and Arabic speaking ones may forget or use their ethnic/religious relationships to secure the individual's 'own' job. Indians' work-related values who work for IBM in Bombay may differ from those who work for a computer company in Silicon Valley or IBM in the US, in spite of the commonly shared organisational structure, due to the nature of the industry.

In fact, value differences across cultures, especially between eastern and western cultures described as individualism versus collectivism have been examined by many scholars for the past two decades. Individualism and collectivism mark the opposing ends of the same cultural value system (Earley, 1993; Ralston et al. 1997). On the other hand, Fijneman et al. (1996) and Moorman and Blakely (1995) support the observed opportunistic view of expatriates working in the Gulf: Westerners, Arabic speakers, Asians, Muslims, Christians and Buddhist alike. As they greatly calculate profit and loss before engaging a behaviour, which is an individualistic approach. On the other hand, the expatriates who originally belong to societies which value membership to a group and look out for the well-being of the group at the expense of their own personal interests may practice this collectivism values once they go back to their countries of origin, and vice-versa. But this assumption needs a further study.

On the other hand, most of the western 'expatriates' in the Gulf can be classified as 'flyers' and 'fighters' in Lasserre's (2003) four Fs', as they generally avoid direct contact with the locals outside work environment. While some, the survivors, may chose to belong to the 'fit' category, as they immerse themselves in the local community. On the other hand, most Asians were observed to 'follow', by adopting the local culture and submitting to it or to the expatriate decision-maker, like in the literary metaphor 'stoop to conquer' of Oliver Goldsmith's famous comedy: She Stoops to Conquer.

C. Uncertainty Avoidance

Uncertainty avoidance refers to managerial behaviours including compliance with social rules formalisation of structure, standardisation of procedures, and centralisation of decision-making. Later, in 1991, Hofstede indicated that the combination of 'uncertainty avoidance' with 'power distance' plays the most significant roles in influencing organizational structure. This combination confirms what is widely observed in many organisations in the Gulf as well as many countries in the Middle East. But this issue requires further investigation.

Accordingly, we may disagree with Dorfman and Howell's (1988) questioning the composition of the uncertainty avoidance dimensions which comprises three different points, as proposed by Hofstede:

a. Length of time the individual believes he or she will work for IBM or other global organisation such as Carrefour and LuLu Hypermarkets in Oman. Perceived stress or stress is also one of the facts of life for most expatriates in the Gulf, as it is difficult to plan for the future due to employment terms. The fear of losing one's job is particularly acute.

b. Whether rules should be broken is the third dimension of Dorfman and Howell's (1988) against Hofstede's. In other words, breaking the rules by bypassing the hierarchical lines in order to have efficient working relationships as indicated by Lasserre (2003) referring to Laurent (1986), is justified, referring to the professional motive of the Nordics and Anglo-Saxons. On the other hand, it was observed that Asian, some Arabic-speaking staff who belong to hierarchical societies may break the rules, but for individualistic rather than professional reasons. This is usually because of their sense of insecurity and being in different work conditions, as described above. In the meantime, many western expatriates may feel frustrated and accordingly they may accept the first alternative or job offer abroad or at home.

D. Masculinity versus Femininity

Table 1.1 indicates that Arabic-speaking countries and Indian societies rank in the middle of the two extremes. As a fact of life, even in the western world today, female students' achievement is higher than males'. In Bahrain and Oman, women are more educated or getting higher degrees than many men.

Generally, the cultural dimensions of Hofstede and others supposed to help applying the person-environment fit concept in multinational employment conditions do not conform to the expatriate employees working environment in different situations, regardless of their cultural or ethnic belonging in Oman or other Gulf countries. Accordingly, further study is required throughout the Gulf countries as the working or employment terms are to some extend similar, in terms of the necessity for the expatriate to have a 'sponsor', its psychological and practical implications and employee's limitations (Jackson, 2003).

E. Other Relevant Cultural Dimensions: Culture and Time

Other dimensions of culture including time value may lead expatriates to misunderstand or not to appreciate some managerial behaviour. For example, dealing with different issues and receiving other people and welcoming them simultaneously, this fits with Hannagan's (2002) reference to Greece as illustrated by Bright and Miller (2005, p. 115), result in lack of appreciation. Allowing such an interruption may seem unprofessional to the new staff, while they perceive these interruptions as a lack of respect, in addition to being contradictory to the organisational culture of an international organisation, e.g. Carrefour in Oman and the Middle East.

Cultural barriers have been explored and identified by earlier research, but the consequences may also vary from one country to another, and also in certain cultures, from one person to another, according to his/her status, social, political influence or even 'ordinary' individuals connected with sources of power. Such consequences might be seen as just a threat to the job security of an expatriate, but in fact, its negative impact will be also on the organisational management, hindering the smooth running of the branch of a global company in similar cultural context.

III. The 'Fit' Concept in the Expatriates' Context

The success of an organisation through the achievement of its objectives depends upon the ability to adapt and 'fit' both among the different organisational components and environmental factors, e.g., culture (Certo, 2000; Edwards and Copper 1990). These are also described, in Chomsky's (1965) terms, as 'deep' or 'surface' meaning and contextual interpretation. Regrettably, many expatriates, managers and staff, who are often seen by some locals as new colonizers, enter and leave these countries without even trying to understand what is beyond the 'surface' meaning of the hesitant, the aggressive or even the polite behaviour or attitude of the locals. This has been observed, either in the multinational contexts which the writer has been part of in Bahrain or Oman, due to the fact that most expatriates are either overwhelmed by their organisational culture and its assumed 'superiority', or live in 'ghettos' keeping a distance from the country's culture and ways of handling simple issues.

The concept 'fit' is defined by Fry's and Smith's theory (1987) as a kind of law of relationship (i.e., congruence) or a system state (i.e., contingency). Accordingly, they suggested that the 'fit' concept is the core of a large number of the organisation and management theories. Venkatraman and Camillus (1984) indicated that this concept is rooted in the population ecology model and its contingency theory tradition which has served as the core force to the development of the middle range theories in many management theories. A proper alignment of the internal design variables is considered an essential pre-requisite to achieving success by contingency theories. This also matches with Fry and Smith (1987, p. 117) inference throughout their review of strategic management, organisation theory and organisation behaviour literature that the concept of 'fit' is:

> "... a particular structure should be matched; technology dictates structure; the environment and strategy should be aligned; internal system should cluster into a way of managing; administrative systems should fit strategy; leader characteristics should be consistent with strategy; and reward system should be congruent with strategy."

Briefly, we can conclude that the concept of 'fit' may represent a type of management objective; either explicit/surface or implicit/deep that usually implies organisational effectiveness (Buchanan and Huczynski, 2004; Drucker, 1967; Mintzberg, 1973 and 1990; Pugh, 1990a and b). The two levels of 'fit' have influenced the organisational and the individual theory. This is in addition to the development of the conceptualisation of congruence quite early in the strategy and organisation design early work (Burns and Stalker, 1961; Chandler, 1962; Pugh, 1990a and b; Woodward, 1965). The concept cultural 'fit' was and will be briefly referred to in this study in terms of the organisational culture and the regional or country's culture dimensions and environmental factors. In this context, it is then necessary to understand how individual employees' values and personality traits influence their attitude towards market orientation (MO). How such attitudes lead to their market-oriented behaviours. In turn, how these behaviours lead to their better individual performance (Gray and Hooley, 2002). To meet its long-term objectives, the company should identify its customer needs and preferences, coordinate a strategic response, and monitor the implementation of this strategic response (Kennedy et al., 2002).

IV. Conclusion

We have shown above the importance of taking into account the concept 'fit' in management in general and in global or even local organisations which employ expatriate managers and staff from different linguistic, geographic, national and cultural backgrounds in different business environment contexts. However, can we only limit the cultural awareness to the organisational behaviour or structure? Or the awareness of cultural diversity (Hofstede, 1989) and the concept 'fit' should be extended to:

1. Human resources management and strategy in employing, rewarding and even penalising. This may raise different issues, including:
   a) The impact of a particular ethnic group culture on global organisation management strategies, e.g. the Indian culture of LuLu Hypermarkets and its influence on non-Indian employees, including Omanis and other nationals in such a global organisation. The emotional, the socio-cultural and the managerial domains are undergoing similar profound changes in Indian managed organisations. For instance, the socio-cultural sphere confronts the dialects of the national macro level reform agenda as well as the challenge of innovating by addressing the hygiene and motivational features of the work place (Chatterjee, 2007).

b) Human resources in a learning organisation (Jackson, 2003; Senge, 1990), particularly in terms of the different backgrounds of the employees and the cost of staff induction and in-service training.

c) Staff orientation given by the local host employer. So, the *Gulf employer, the franchised Carrefour Hypermarkets* (Carrefour Group in the Gulf) and the global retailer *Lulu Hypermarkets* (EMKE Group in the Gulf) *in the Gulf or even the Middle East,* when employing Europeans, Omanis, Arabs, Indians and staff from other countries should ensure that their employees 'fit' in the corporate organisation culture to conform to the organisational culture and meet its quality standards.

d) This raises many questions to be answered in terms of not only the parent company organisational culture, but also the culture of the countries where the subsidiaries or branches are located, as well as the diversified cultures of the management and employees which result in different styles of management and marketing strategies.

e) Staff motivation, commitment, organisation's culture, and structure organisation as well as leadership (Bass, 1985; Bass and Avolio, 1994; Hofstede, 1994 and 1996; Stogdill, 1974) and their impact on the marketing strategies.

f) Identifying and meeting customer needs and wants by adopting and monitoring the strategy which meets the firm's goals and objectives. In so doing, recruiting the right calibre of employees with values and personality traits that influence their attitudes towards MO is a pre-requisite to meeting such needs and realising the firm's objectives.

Briefly, all the above-mentioned issues including organisational culture, diversity of backgrounds of employed human resources and the local context, e.g., Oman will naturally influence marketing decisions and strategies. In other words, marketing management in its broader sense including advertising, pricing, the type and quality services, and opening new hypermarkets will be influenced. Other issues might also influence the hypermarkets marketing strategies such as the sudden rise of oil prices, the rise of the rate of inflation, particularly in region, as most of their currencies' value has been practically devalued, due to the declining value of the US dollars. In fact, this has a great impact on the prices of food products in countries which import most of their food products needs. So, how would these retailers react? What marketing strategies would they adopt or have to adopt in such a turbulent business environment where not only food products have been inflated, but also buildings rents, including staff accommodation? Indeed, such questions need to be addressed.

2 Cultural Diversity and Marketing Strategies

I. The Impact of Globalisation on Marketing Strategies

Strolling through a bustling souk [market] - whether in Muscat or a small village - is an invigorating experience. With many sellers, you know you will get the best price and the best quality.

> "Every seller knows they are [sic] in competition with every seller, so each struggles to find the best price …. It's not just the sellers; the producers also have the buyers in mind. They too realise they face a competitive market place."
>
> McMahon, Director, Centre for Globalisation Studies, The Fraser Institute (2006, p. 21)

Indeed, it is a challenge for marketers, e.g., global retailers, as well as global companies including producers, providing services and/or employers of expatriates of different cultures, ethnic backgrounds, in addition to the national or local employees, to find the right proportion or the right mix to 'fit' between:

a) Competitive performance, including producing and selling quality goods and services at competitive prices (Berry and Parasuraman, 1991).

b) Maximising the potential of the organisation's 'tangible' and 'intangible' resources, in an environment, Oman, the Gulf countries or the Middles East, where it is difficult to protect resources, products or services [including intellectual property] from imitation (Collis and Montgomery, 1995).

c) Individual and organisational patterns of behaviour, value systems and marketing strategies (Brislin, 2000).

d) Organisational structure and contingency variables, i.e., in environmental adjustment or 'fit' of leaders, personnel and organisations to the environment and culture within which they exist and have to compete and maximise the market capabilities (Fahy et al., 2000).

A. Globalisation Labelling and Definitions

In order to review and analyse the differences and similarities in the practices of marketing in global businesses, it is necessary to define marketing concepts which refer to important factors influencing marketing strategies (Doyle, 1998). Indeed, globalisation and its impact led to different definitions by prominent scholars, CEOs and marketers by giving it different labels including 'global industries', 'global competition', 'global strategies', 'global corporations' and 'multinational companies' (Hill, 2000 and 2003).

Briefly, the above mentioned globalisation labels or definitions simplify such complex processes and strategies. For example, let us compare the penetration of the retailer 'Carrefour' in the Gulf and then the Middle East which required active coordination not only with Carrefour's Head Offices in France or the UAE, but also with different local and regional partners (Prahalad and Hamel, 1990). This is in addition to other management and marketing strategies which imply thorough insights, cultural awareness, challenges, risks and maximising the use of 'tangible' and 'intangible' resources (Hunt and Morgan, 1996; Keegan, 1995).

B. Marketing Definitions

Marketing may also be defined as "a corporate state of mind that insists on the integration and coordination of all of the marketing functions which, in turn, are melted with other corporate functions, for the basic objective of producing maximum long-range corporate profits" (Felton, 1959, p. 55). It was also defined as the external consumer orientation and the complete integration of organisational and operational effort having profit targets rather than sales volume. Palmer and Hartley (1996, p. 1) quoting Dibb et al. (1994) indicated that "marketing consists of individual organisational activities that facilitate and expedite satisfying exchange relationships in a dynamic environment through the creation, distribution, promotion and pricing of goods, services and ideas." Needham and Dransfield (1995, p.1) referring to the Chartered Institute of Marketing's definition described it as "...

the management process responsible for identifying, anticipating and satisfying consumer requirements profitably." On the other hand, Kotler and Keller (2006, p. 6) regard marketing management "... as the art and science of choosing target markets and getting, keeping and growing customers through creating, delivering and communicating superior customer value."

The above-mentioned definitions lead us to conclude that marketing comprises:
  a) Defining business products, services and target markets in close collaboration with other departments including R&D, production, finance and HR, as well as suppliers.
  b) Promoting and delivering these products and/or services to ultimate users at the lowest cost possible and highest perceived value for the customers.
  c) Being aware of the dynamic marketing environment which influences the creation, networks, distribution, promotion, pricing of goods, services ideas and maximising the use of processing information as an asset which influences marketing decisions.

In conclusion, global organisation's management and marketers should not only be aware of the customer's behaviour, needs, wants and desires but also sometimes educate the customers, create a new need or replace a present one. In my view, this process includes eight, not five, **Ps**: Positioning and background information, *Product, Pricing, Promotion, Place*, and additional marketing mix including *People, Process, Personal* services and quality, and *Processing information*, Appendix D. It summarises the findings of the pilot study conducted in September 2006-January 2007, of the five global retailers' in Oman and the Middle East with particular reference to asset-based theory, competitiveness and extended marketing mix.

II. Maximising the Potential of the Organisation and Competitive Performance

As the focus of this case study is the *franchised* retailer Carrefour as well as the global retailer LuLu Hypermarkets, issues dealing with global firms' management and marketing strategies, cultural diversity as well as human resources implications are reviewed. Global companies generally tend to manage a group of firms or 'foreign subsidiaries' in an integrated and coordinated way out of their head offices or countries of origin. This view or style of management is in line with the theories of many scholars including Doz et al. (2002), Hunt and Morgan (1996), as well as Prahalad and Doz, (1987). They suggested the terms 'transnationals' or 'metanational' firms to describe such new entities, which Yip (1992) called the 'Global Strategy'. Accordingly, more emphasis throughout this empirical study is on local culture(s) and consequently entry and marketing strategies as well as the expatriate management. Accordingly the management is expected to 'think globally and act locally.'

Theoretically, a company becoming global results in more success and higher levels of profitability. On the other hand, the management and marketing strategies imply more challenges and risks. Accordingly, the management and the marketing strategies of a global company armed with a brand and the know-how have to take into account the following:

a) The need for a thorough analysis of competitors in collaboration with other functions, such as products, R&D, finance, local and regional suppliers.

b) The need to be equipped with analysis of the dynamic and volatile business environment retail business in Oman or any other country which should include anticipations about current and long-term trends in demand.

c) The need for data analysis and awareness of the other functions, including networks, understanding and predicting the situation on the market and the behaviour of their target customers as well as their needs (Greenley and Foxall, 1997 and 1998).

d) The development of specific techniques such as advertising, promotion and management of sales force in the most efficient manner to ensure having a market competitive advantage.

e) The concern that all activities contribute to the profitability of the business, whether being a retailer, a producer or a supplier.

In so doing, increasing the customer's 'perceived' value, the implementation of a sustainable resource-based view will be realised through the examination of the organisation's alternative opportunities through the increasing of the customer's benefits and/or decreasing its acquisition and usage costs by calculating the cost of each step from R&D to production and distribution (Grant, 1991 and 1995). Research and development may also find new product(s), more efficient production and marketing strategies which add value to perceived products and services (Crouch and Housden, 1996). Learning organisations may regard human resources as an asset resulting in a non-duplicating competitive asset. Therefore, they would recruit, train, reward and motivate the personnel in such an ethical way that it would become a key factor in the search for lower cost and higher perceived value (Barney 1991; Bharadwaj et al. 1993; Dessler, 2001; Porter, 1985, 1986 and 1996). Accordingly:

a) Global positioning and competitiveness are also key issues related to successful analysis of market dynamics and prediction of new markets and market needs (Conner, 1995).

b) Sustaining having a competitiveness advantage ethically helps maintaining a competitive edge.

c) It should be noted that a global company should sustain its market orientation (MO), competitive performance, successfully implement the resource-based theory and competitively 'fit' between selected market targets in developing countries.

d) To maximise competencies and the use of tangible and intangible assets, the marketing team as well as other functions which need to have an understanding of the market through market research and other market information or *intelligence*.

e) It is then up to the marketing group to make customers aware of the competitive advantages of the products, services as well as R&D and finance.

Briefly, the marketer should know far beyond market research about the market and about his company and its products as well as services. It should be also realised that customers are not necessarily good sources of data about their needs in a few months, not to mention a decade from now. They do not know how they will react under different environmental conditions, such as booms, crisis or recession. Customers usually do not have insight into possible value of major technological changes, social beliefs and ways of behaving (Houston, 1986). This implies that business must also invent, innovate and test products and services without clear advanced knowledge and try to have these products and services meet needs, wants and desires, which are only emerging or have not yet been well identified.

It should also be noted that customers' behaviour and needs are influenced by different environmental or market circumstances where each of the functions of a business can have alternatively a predominant role. For example, during a period of economic recession, financial considerations tend to dominate the customers' decisions as well as the company's. At a time of vast technological changes or business boom, production and R&D activities might have a bigger weight on decisions. On the other hand, in a growing and highly competitive market, marketing strategies seem to have the biggest impact. Briefly, the marketing practices are positively or negatively influenced by many elements, which are dynamic and sometimes unpredictable.

That explains the discrepancy in defining marketing concepts between academicians, CEOs and marketers in many different ways, to the extent that similarities, nuances and even divergences are usually found among these definitions.

III. Marketing Strategies and Marketing Orientation

In conclusion, from the points of view of this case study and the other examples mentioned above, there are five interrelated levels according to which marketing strategies, organisation and practices have to be formed from company to company and from time to time due to the market dynamics and the changing environmental factors with particular reference to fast cultural changes which affect customers' perceived values. These are:

a) Company level
b) Business or industry level
c) Environment level
d) Marketing orientation
e) Consumer level

Managers and marketers, when establishing a marketing strategy, should take into account the factors that relate to these five levels, particularly when operating in different businesses or industries, environments or countries. Companies which operate in the same business, such as the retailers and within the same environment might be confronted by many consumer behaviours, as is the case of the western and Omani customers' behaviour versus the working class and sometimes the middle class Asian expatriates in Oman. Marketers have to understand consumers' behaviour in order to identify segments or niches which will be the most profitable for the sale of their products and services, by predicting and applying the right mix to 'fit' in the culture's and market's contexts. In addition,

> "... being a Marketer means that there are no new ideas just variations on a theme, the substitution of thought for dispute and debate, of knowledge for publicity and propaganda and communication for hype and hyperbole. And if, while reading this piece you thought 'some of this is a rewording of old stuff', well hey, that's marketing."
>
> Punt (2006, p. 55)

On the other hand, the *impact of cultural issues on marketing strategies* should be taken seriously, as culture is present at the four levels and has a reciprocal influence along with other factors at each level, as the customer is the core of the entire process including satisfying his/her needs, and wants at a competitive level (Day, 1994; Day and Nedungadi, 1994; Leonard-Barton, 1992; Schoemaker, 1992). Organisations should also ensure having "… the ability to identify opportunities and then select appropriate market targets where the firm's resources and capabilities are aligned to optimum effect." Hooley et al. (1998, p. 103). But the deployment of hard to imitate products and services (Prahalad and Hamel, 1990) seems difficult to realise not only in China, but also in developing countries, including Gulf countries which claim protecting property rights. It is also hard to maintain innovation and consequently superior competitiveness and performance for long. For example, we mention duplicated CDs and DVDs which can be bought for less than one and a half pound sterling (one Bahraini Dinar or one Omani Riyal) in Ruwi High Street in Muscat. One can also get 100 ml/3.4 oz of copied Chanel No 5 eau de parfum from the Souk of Bab Al Bahrain in Manama for the same cost. This is also referred to in relation to core capabilities and the paradox in new product development (Leonard-Barton, 1992) and ways to maintain superior performance (Olavarrieta and Friedmann, 1999). On the other hand, if brands and products can be imitated or replicated, having a satisfied well-trained staff, but not necessarily with unique or rare capabilities, however, being able to manage and initialise their diversity is the key to maximise the use of resources and to have a competitive edge which cannot be imitated or cloned.

In addition, the important element of employees' satisfaction needs as well as person-fit have to be addressed in the retail business and other global organisations. This is to ensure that staff and marketers are fairly compensated for the work performed. In so doing, the organisations' overall pay structure needs to be professionally and/or ethically reviewed. This would be one of the positive ways organisations can use pay to recognise individual and group contributions to the firm's performance, as well as ensuring the employees' natural and positive interaction with customers, resulting in higher perceived value of products and services as well as organisational cohesion, marketing change and innovation prediction in the right direction (Blyton and Turnbull, 1996; Bratton and Gold, 2003; Kamoche; 1996, Miller, 1990). Indeed, MO is an important element to meet customers' needs and preferences by coordinating a strategic response and monitoring the implementation of this strategic response (Gray and Hooley, 2002; Kennedy et al, 2002).

IV. Conclusion: From Theory to Practice

This results in maximising the global company's resource-based assets including tangible and intangible resources. So, the firm becomes highly competitive even in a dynamic and volatile market environment, e.g., Oman and other Gulf countries due to the higher cost of imported food products, as these countries import most of these products, the devaluation of most Gulf currencies which are tied to the US dollar, and the recent aggressive marketing strategies of the LuLu supermarkets (EMKE Group) including the threats of opening of new hypermarkets in many regions in Oman and Gulf countries within few months. Lately, this has been experienced by Gulf consumers mostly by the rising inflation rate. Due to taking into account market trends, market orientation strategy and being able to be quicker in responding to customers' needs:

a) The global LuLu Hypermarket Group (EMKE Group) has become the market leader in Oman in the Gulf, its market share is 32%.

b) While Carrefour's market share has unexpectedly become 14% only.

c) Spinny's market share is 11%

d) Other retailers' share is 28%, as indicated by Godo Research and Marketing Consultancy (2008).

Accordingly, the focus of this study was mainly on the market leader, LuLu, and its main competitor in Oman, Carrefour, with some reference to other global and local retailers' influences. These retailers are:

a) Carrefour Hypermarkets and Shopping Centres (Global French-Franchised Owned by an Emirati Group) – used to be the market leader, in Oman.

b) Lulu Hypermarkets and Supermarkets (Global South Indian EMKE Group), has become the market leader.

c) Al Safeer Hypermarket and Supermarkets (Gulf Company Owned by an Emirati Group).
d) The Sultan Center & Supermarket (Al Jumlah) (Gulf Company Owned by a Kuwaiti Group).
e) Al Fair Supermarkets (Global Spinneys' Franchised Group, Owned by an Emirati Group).

To identify the conceptual framework and the factors influencing the marketing strategies of the five global retailers in Oman the following factors were addressed in detail in the pilot study, see findings in Appendix D. These factors include:

a) The role of marketing as conceived by the management
b) The size the activities of the retailer in relation to the other retailers
c) The company structure and the organisational culture impact
d) The kind of products/services mix
e) The financial situation, in terms of being able to compete or even survive in such a highly competitive market
f) The human resources, including the impact of the recruiting system, the quality of service, staff attitude due to organisation culture and the staff cultural background in Gulf context
g) The technological resources, which have been playing an effective role
h) The competitive situation taking into account the high inflation rate due to sudden rise in the food products' prices, e.g. rice, milk, wheat
i) The retailers' values, objectives and strategies.

In fact, the impact of the marketing mix does not only include the quality, variety and the price of the products, the promotion strategies and the place (convenience) which were the most influential factors, but also people and marketing mix including recruiting system, staff attitude, loyalty, and commitment, quality of service, use of information technology/processing information and the conceived role of management as well as the important role of the top management/leadership. To meet such a challenge, the management and the marketing people should have the skills that equip them with the tools to understand the environment, the industry, the company, the market and above all the consumer. That means that, as individuals, they should have managerial competencies, such as communication skills, analytical strategic thinking as well as enough judgement and intuition to be sensitive to customers' present and future needs and wants.

In conclusion, the findings of Kashani (1996) where more than 200 general managers and marketing executives indicated that organisations are becoming aware that an effective and more influential way of making and monitoring strategic decisions is everybody's business in the company, rather than being confined to a separate function. In other words, companies increasingly resort to interdisciplinary groups or teams in which managers and staff share together, on equal footing, their experience and knowledge. Indeed, firms are likely to conceive different options or solutions as regards the status of marketing, with periodical reviews and adjustments, as it is the case of LuLu Hypermarkets (EMKE Group), in search for responses which, in the present turbulent local and global markets, might be only temporary. Briefly, marketing is perceived today as a staff function and more of an operational activity in which people, with a variety of backgrounds, horizons and viewpoints are aware of what the different markets are.

In conclusion, companies including global retailers have to continually assess and manage today's complex market environment through not only HRD, but also to maximise the use of innovative technology and information processing in a globally integrated platform. Adopting a broad-based systematic approach to marketing issues within the global marketplace with its different environments, cultures and customers' identified, predicted and created needs leads to outstanding performance and making better use of the variety of resources of the respective firm resulting in having an outstanding competitive advantage, which is not easy to imitate. Accordingly, the above-mentioned conceptual framework for understanding the factors influencing the retail industry marketing strategies in Oman will be evaluated in this study through the present study quantitative and qualitative data collection sources using management, staff, customers, observations and documents to discuss, analyse and evaluate the findings in the following chapters.

3 Identifying the Effects of cultural Diversity on Global Companies' Marketing Strategies, Human Resources Management

I. Background and Rationale of the Study

The purpose of these two case studies was to identify the effects of cultural diversity on global companies' corporate behaviour, management, as well as marketing strategies. Therefore, the two major global retailers in Oman, Carrefour and Lulu Hypermarkets, were selected as the focus of the study. Other global/international and local hypermarkets or supermarkets were also referred to.

II. The Conceptual Framework and Study Questions

A. Conceptual Framework

The global companies' model of management in the Gulf and the Middle East and its economic growth has received considerable attention since the seventies, the starting of the rise of oil prices and its direct economic impact on the region. This has opened new markets for global companies which resulted in many challenges in terms of:
1. The global companies' corporate behaviour and the cultural and sub-cultural diversity of the region, due to religious, political and economical variables.
2. The need to employ local staff and expatriates in addition to the employees of the companies' management of their countries of origin. This results in a cultural diversity and its impact on the companies' style of management, corporate behaviour and marketing strategies.

3. The need to creatively modify products to meet the needs, wants, desires and even aspiration of the potential customers.

4. When outer directed and facing foreign lands and competitors, the country and the companies gather their 'resources' with the aim to win the contest. In so doing, global food and technology suppliers have to adopt aggressive policies in the field of international trade, direct manufacturing and financial investments abroad, i.e. Oman and its neighbouring countries.

5. Although global companies 'secrets' have generally been identified in manufacturing, their implementations have not been without effects on the marketing function. The growing flow of new products and the concepts of 'speed to the market' or 'first to the market' meant that the marketing groups had little time to indulge themselves in extensive market research. Taking into account cultural awareness, this should not only be limited to the products but also be extended to other 'tangible' and 'intangible' resources including HRM and training (Collis and Montgomery 1995).

B. Study Questions

Accordingly, the following study questions were addressed:
1. What about the marketing approaches applied in the global companies' countries of origin, can they 'fit' the conditions of the countries? What have been the responses of the global companies in Oman?

2. Global companies seem to have applied several of their management practices to their subsidiaries and they must also have used there their home marketing techniques. Have these global companies adjusted their specifications to the practices and needs of the host country, Oman?

3. Then, do these global companies have to review and even adapt their marketing strategies in response to the global competition and above all the local culture of the host countries and their diversities?

4. As many global companies, such as the European and Japanese appear to have gained inspirations from North

American marketing models and practices, would this suggest a progressive approximation of marketing policies, with whenever possible, original solutions reflecting the corporate culture of each global company, as well as its products and specific markets, i.e. Oman?

5. Is the concept of market orientation (MO) taken into consideration when planning and implementing a marketing strategy? (Gray and Hooley, 2002). In so doing, are the customers' needs, wants and satisfaction taken into consideration by Carrefour and LuLu? Are the staff satisfaction, attitude, commitment and performance; financial or marketing performance; and innovation taken into consideration when planning and implementing policies? (Deshpandé, Farley, and Webster, 1993; Homburg and Pflesser, 2000; Jaworski and Kohli, 1996; Narver and Slater, 1990; Slater and Narver, 1994).

6. Could these analyses lead to some general conclusions on the more recent evolution of marketing theories and practices in particular contexts, such as developing countries or emerging markets?

7. In such a specific or foreign context where products and even brands are instantly imitated or replicated, would these global companies give more emphasis on satisfying and training their employees, not necessarily with unique or rare capabilities? So, firms can manage and utilise their diversity as the key to maximise the use of resources and to have a competitive edge, particularly in the retail industry, which cannot be imitated or cloned, as it is the case with products (Porter, 1980, 1996).

8. In other words, will the concept a person-environment fit, independent from its background, result in positive individual or organisational outcomes, such as satisfaction and organisational commitment? (Edwards, 1996; Edwards and Rothbard, 1999).

Hypotheses of the Study

This study made use of the null hypothesis throughout the study. No significant difference, 0.05 level of significance, with response(s) to the choices made in each item on the global companies' staff's and customers' questionnaires were applicable.

H.1. There is no significant difference between Omani and non-Omani customers in perceiving customers' needs and/or criteria, as well as their perceptions of marketing strategies in Oman, such as:
   a) Low prices as well as variety of brands, quality of products and prices
   b) Different types of discounts
   c) Raffles and prizes as well as earning points and reward cards
   d) Special products and convenient location
   e) Quality of service

H.2. There is no significant difference between the Omani and non-Omani customers in their perception of the marketing strategies, including the quality of products or the variety of brands and prices, as well as the quality of service provided by Carrefour and LuLu hypermarkets in Oman.

H3. There is no significant difference between the perceptions of the Omani and non-Oman customers' perceptions in terms of the quality of services received as well as their availability in their favourite hypermarkets/supermarkets: Carrefour, LuLu or others.

H.4. There is no significant difference between the organisation culture and the style of management of both the Global retailers in Oman, i.e., Carrefour and LuLu Hypermarkets, as perceived by their respective staff.

H.5. There is no significant difference between the staff's *level of satisfaction* of Carrefour and LuLu Hypermarkets' with their organisation culture and the style of management.

H.6. There is no significant difference between policies when dealing with 'intangible' resources, such as human resources and their training as well as recruitment in global companies' countries of origin, and in the host countries.

III. Main and Secondary Data Sources

The study opted for the triangulation of research instruments, data and sources using quantitative and qualitative test instruments. Accordingly, the following test instruments were used:

1. Questionnaires:
   a) *Customers' Questionnaire*, Appendix A, accompanied by semi-structured interviews. It aimed at identifying the Omani and the non-Omani customers' needs and/or criteria as well as perceptions, such as prices, brands, location convenience, perceived good value for money, availability of special products, quality of service, and their perceptions of the marketing strategies adopted by their favourite hypermarket/supermarket.
   b) *Management and Staff Questionnaire*, for Carrefour and LuLu Hypermarkets staff, Appendix B. It comprised twenty objective questions on a five level scale and two open-ended questions seeking additional information and suggestions. Its purpose was to identify the different levels' of staff's perception of the way their organisation is managed and the way they wish it to be. The questionnaire also aimed at identifying the staff's attitude towards their company. An Arabic version of both questionnaires was made available for Arabic speakers, following the validation of the original English version.

2. *Semi-Structured Interviews for Global Retailers and Suppliers*, managerial staff of Carrefour (6), and LuLu (15) as well as two representatives of Nestlé, Unilever, Sony, Canon, Toshiba and HP. It comprised thirty one questions, Appendix C. The raised questions were meant too seek additional information and clarifications of issues raised by customers and staff. The use of semi-structured interviews, which also have their subjectivity problems, with managers, staff, and customers for other purposes including filling the gaps of the questionnaires and their limitations (Antonakis et al., 2003; Blyton, 2001; Duffy, 1987; Gaulis, 1996; Jick, 1983; LeCompte and Goetz, 1982; Simon, Vosseberg and Levett, 2001).

3. *Observations* as a useful and complementary tool, in spite of its subjectivity too, was expected to help integrating and analysing the overall results.

4. *Materials, data and documents* which supported the
   documentary analysis were mainly from local, regional and
   international newspapers, magazines, government documents,
   booklets, reports, yearly statistic reports and leaflets produced by the
   Ministry of Manpower and the Ministry of National Economy and
   websites. This is in addition to having access to the Ministry of
   Manpower database, as one of its employees.

Construction and selection of the test instruments

In designing the questionnaires, a common pattern was followed
as far as possible so that information obtained could be checked
directly point by point to determine whether there was any
substantial agreement or disagreement on any particular point
between the groups (managers, staff, marketers, suppliers, and
customers), Appendices A-C. In the meantime, the research was
based on a comparative analysis taking into consideration the
global companies' countries of origin, and the host countries,
mainly Oman and some countries in the Gulf and the Middle East,
where applicable. This involved economic, cultural, social and
political factors. Accordingly, the study relied on an empirical
and a conceptual body of knowledge, attitudes, beliefs and
practices that have their roots in the past. This may justify a
number of comments on the backgrounds of the selected global
companies, i.e., as Carrefour and LuLu as well as their global
suppliers.

Validation of Questionnaires and Development of Semi-Structured Interviews Questions

a) The first draft of the questionnaire was piloted using few
   members of academic staff, marketers and customers seeking
   suggestions to clear any misconceptions or misinterpretations,
   to be included in the final version.
b) On the other hand, the development of list of questions of the
   semi-structure interviews was an on-going process since August
   2006. It was based upon the collected documents, observations
   and the piloted semi-structured interviews conducted with
   representatives of the following global companies based in
   Switzerland and other bodies in Canton Vaud: Chambre

Vaudoise du Commerce et de l'Industrie; Nestlé; Tetra Pak Export S.A.; Siemens.

c) The initial qualitative data collection in the form of semi-structured interviews, analysis of corporate data and documents and observations at Carrefour, LuLu, their global and local competitors and global suppliers in Oman. Briefly, Appendix D, summarises the findings of the pilot study which helped not only in the initial design of the test instruments but also in deciding the study limitations, to include only Carrefour Hypermarket as the market leader, and LuLu Hypermarkets, as its first competitor in Oman.

The final versions of the two questionnaires were developed in English because it is the major language and the most commonly used by global firms and retailers. They were then translated into Arabic; the back-translation technique was then applied (Brislin, 1970; 1976). The translation was double checked by customers, retail staff and specialists. So, the translation/adaptation process took full account of linguistic and cultural differences among the populations for whom the translated versions of instruments was intended. This was done bearing in mind Roberts' (1970) view that techniques such as back-translation are only minimum conditions for cross-cultural research. Therefore, problems may still arise when no good translation equivalents can be found, especially when words have to be translated out of context (Osgood, 1967; cited in Drenth and Groenendijk, 1984, p. 1201).

IV. The Study Sample

The sample for the main study comprised:

a) 838 randomly selected customers from different areas of Muscat. The data was collected by some of the students of the Higher College of Technology, Muscat, according to their different residential areas, Table 3.1. It should be noted that 123 incomplete questionnaires were excluded, to avoid any false statistical significance. Table 4.1 groups the study sample according to the nearest hypermarkets/supermarkets per closest geographical area or region. Natural representation of the different ethnic groups of Omanis and expatriates was observed. They answered the "Customer Questionnaire", Appendix A.

b) The "Staff Questionnaire: Business Cultural Values", Appendix B, was answered by 113 managers and staff working for Carrefour and LuLu. The researcher requested permission from the management, but kept a low profile and made use of his good relationship, as an employee of the Ministry of Manpower. Tables 3.2-3.4 classify staff by nationality, level of education and training and job level.

c) Top and middle managers of Carrefour (6) and LuLu (15) as well as two of each of their suppliers of global products, i.e. Nestlé, Unilever, Sony, Canon, and HP located in Muscat, Oman, were interviewed. They answered the "Semi-Structured Interviews for Global Retailers and Suppliers in Oman", Appendix C.

Table 3.1: Customers' Study Sample Grouped by Omani and Non-Omani*

Omani	Non-Omani	Total
N=431	N=407	N=838*
51.43%	48.57%	100%
	(110 westerners, 118 Arabs and 179 Asians)	

* Table 4.1 groups the study sample by regions and main competitive hypermarkets/supermarkets

Table 3.2: Grouping of the Staff Study Sample by Nationality

Nationality	Carrefour	Lulu
Omani	10	12
Arabs	20	16
Indians	18	22
Asians (Philippines & others)	5	8
Others	0	2
Total	53	60

Table 3.3: Grouping of the Staff Study Sample by Level of Education and Training

Nationality	Carrefour	Lulu
Secondary School Certificate, Technical Diploma	42	25
Vocational Training (GNVQ, NVQ), Higher Technical Diploma	6	5
BSc., BA	2	18
MBA, MA	3	12
Total	53	60

Table 3.4: Grouping of the Staff Study Sample
by Job Level

Nationality	Carrefour	Lulu
Non-Management	40	32
Lower Management	7	13
Middle Management	4	12
Top Management	2	3
Total	53	60*

* LuLu's managerial staff was more accessible and secure than Carrefour's

V. Data Analysis Technique

Quantitative and qualitative analyses were used including:
   a) Frequency of each response of all questionnaire questions.
   b) Chi-square ($\chi 2$) test, where necessary to compare test significance of differences between choices of one item and between groups, staff and customers. Null hypothesis was rejected for $p \leq 0.05$.
   c) Mean score for some of the items of the questionnaires.
   d) *Two-tailed* t-test was also used to identify the differences between the two means of the responses of the "Staff Questionnaire: Business Cultural Values", Appendix A, due to the small size of the sample, 113. However, it was not be used to analyse the "Customer Questionnaire", Appendix A, due to the large size of the sample (Hatch and Farhady, 1982). This is because with large-size samples, the values of t critical and z critical will be almost identical.
   e) The integration of the qualitative data analysis of the semi-structured interviews, observations as well as documents with the analysis and interpretation of the quantitative data.

VI. *The Scope of the Study, its Limitations and Conclusion*

Accordingly, this study was limited to the retail industry in Oman, mainly:

a) LuLu hypermarkets and its major competitors in Oman Carrefour, with *brief reference*, where applicable, to other global retail competitors in Oman and countries.

b) Some of Carrefour' and LuLu's retailers' global suppliers in Oman, i.e. Sony, Canon, Toshiba, HP, Nestlé and Unilever.

On one hand, using the *quantitative data collection test instrument*, i.e. *questionnaires*, is a powerful tool in collecting data from a wide range of population and in facilitating data processing and analysis. But, it is considered rigid and restrictive in its limited contextual information processing ability. In addition, several responses bias (e.g., social desirability bias, common method bias) might also reduce the *reliability* of its results. Therefore, the *qualitative data collection methods*, i.e. semi-structured interviews in conjunction with observations as well as collection of materials and documents, were viewed to be necessary to collect more credible results auditing and deeper analyses purposes. This was not only due to the obvious limitations of the questionnaire as a quantitative test instrument, but also because of two other reasons (Antonakis et al., 2003; Blyton, 2001; Duffy, 1987; Gaulis, 1996; Jick, 1983; LeCompte and Goetz, 1982; Simon, Vosseberg and Levett, 2001):

a) The nature of the retail industry and the wild competitive market which might either impede the use of this instrument or provide limited or biased data.

b) Most of the target audience consists of both Asians (mainly Indians) and Arabic speaking staff who generally belong to the power-distance groups (Hofstede, 1980; 1990).

These limitations were also enhanced by most of the employees and even some of the retail industry clients' low socio-economic groups of expatriates feeling insecure regarding their employment due to the working conditions and terms in Oman and the Gulf. However, as observed during the piloting stage, some can speak their minds and be outspoken once they trust the interviewer and his 'motives'.

Accordingly, it is recommended not to overestimate the value of written data or personally recorded data of the questionnaire for the validity of the results. Therefore, some qualitative instruments were used to ensure triangulation of tools, sources, documents and data for more *reliable* and *valid* findings.

Data Analysis and Results I:

4 Customers' Needs and Perceptions of Marketing Strategies in a Multicultural Context

I. Introduction and the Approach for the Two Case Studies

Chapters 3-6 analyse two case studies of two global retailers in Oman: The French franchised Carrefour Hypermarket, a Dubai, United Arab Emirates (UAE) based, Majid Al Futtaim (MAF); and LuLu Hypermarkets, an Abu Dhabi UAE-based EMKE South Indian Group, in Oman. Both case studies aim at analysing the retail industry in Oman in order to examine the impact of cultural diversity and global management on marketing strategies. Accordingly, the following analysis divides the market orientation elements into two main groups:

a) Customers' needs, wants and satisfaction and their perceptions of marketing strategies, this chapter.

b) Staff satisfaction, attitude, commitment and performance; marketing performance and innovation, Chapter 5.

The data collection of the *Customer Questionnaire*, Appendix A, was administered by some students of the Higher College of Technology (HCT), under the umbrella of the Ministry of Manpower, according to their residential areas in Muscat and Al Batinah region. These are where *Carrefour, LuLu* have their hypermarkets,. The total number of the analysed questionnaires was 838; Table 4.1. The total number of completed questions in the questionnaire may vary due to the nature of the question, bearing in mind that an additional 123 incomplete questionnaires were excluded to avoid any false statistical significance.

II. Consumer Retail Hypermarkets and Products

A wide range of traditional consumer retail products are found under one roof in the cases of the two retailers. Oman Economic Review (2008) indicates the challenges the Omani retail and food market face, where most products are imported, as the inflation rate rose to 12.4% in Oman. So, which retailer(s) would be able to respond faster to such challenges?

Therefore, some retailers produce and pack their own products and have recently increased the volume and variety of production for overseas, for example:

a) Most of LuLu's managers reported that he EMKE Group, "ventured into varied businesses operating in the UAE, Oman, Qatar, Kuwait, Bahrain, Saudi Arabia, Yemen, India, Indonesia, Thailand, Hong Kong, China, Kenya, Tanzania and Benin". This was also verified, as the writer was shown LuLu's/the EMKE's own products ranging from food, to garment and Ikon electronic products, under different brand names as well as LuLu's own brand name. Moreover, it was reported that "since 2007 the variety of LuLu brands has suddenly increased in the form of family size packages, in order to lower the prices to combat the rise of food and other products prices. This was the fastest response to customers' needs in Oman". Furthermore, when acquiring or packing many products, LuLu has copied Nestlé's marketing strategy, by maintaining the original brand's name and discreetly adding LuLu's logo. So, LuLu maintains the added value of the original brand names.

b) On the other hand, Carrefour's managers failed to provide any evidence in response to the economic situation. It continued producing its regular brands without responding to price inflation, customer needs or the threats of the emerging local markets competition. This could be due to the fact that the Carrefour brand names are produced to meet the needs of the global market, rather than the Omani or Gulf markets.

Table 4.1: Grouping of Hypermarkets/Supermarkets According to the Closest Geographical Area or Region

Regions	Omani	Non-Omani	Total	The Major Clustered/Nearest Hypermarkets/Supermarkets & Remarks
Muscat				
1 Mattrah, Darsait, Ruwi	N=76 65.52%	N=40 34.48% (1 westerner, 1 Arab & 38 Asians)	N=116 100%	**LuLu** (Darsait), **El Osra Supermarket**, Ruwi, and **Al Fair Supermarket** (Spinneys), Ruwi.
2 Al Quorum, Al Sarouj, Al Ealaam	N=70 37.63%	N=116 6237% (32 westerners, 40 Arabs & 44 Asians)	N=186 100%	**LuLu** (Baushar), **Sultan Centre** (Al Quorum), **Al Fair Supermarket** (MQ), (Al Quorum), **Al Fair** (Al Sarouj) **Al Fair Supermarket** (Khuwair, *closed down following the opening of LuLu*) and **Carrefour Hyper.**
3 North & South Ghubra, Ghala, Al Azaiba and Al Khuwair	N=74 41.11%	N=106 58.89% (33 westerners, 35 Arabs & 38 Asians)	N=180 100%	**LuLu Hypermarket** (Baushar), **Al Safeer Hypermarket** (The main Branch) and **Pick and Save Supermarket** (Al Safeer).
4 Al Hail and Al Seeb	N=96 49.74%	N=97 50.26% (30 westerners, 30 Arabs & 37 Asians)	N=193 100%	**Carrefour** (Seeb), **Al Jumlah Hypermarket** (opened following the opening of Carrefour in Seeb, a branch of Sultan Centre), Then, **Al Burge Supermarket** (acquired recently by **LuLu** in Seeb). **Both are close to Carrefour.**
Total	N=316 46.81%	N=359 53.19% (96 westerners, 106 Arabs & 157 Asians)	N=675 100%	
Al Batinah Region (The highest density of the Omani population in the country)*				
5 North and South Al Mubeela, and Barka	N=115 70.55%	N=48 29.45% (14 westerners, 12 Arabs & 22 Asians)	N=163 100%	**LuLu Hypermarket** (Barka), **Al Tayeb Supermarket, Al Baraka Supermarket**. The population is mainly Omanis and a very low percentage of expatriates*
Grand Total	N=431 51.43%	N=407/ 48.57% (110 westerners, 118 Arabs & 179 Asians)	N=838 100%	**Muscat & Al Batinah Regions**

*Ministry of National Economy (2004)

III. Cultural Diversity: Customers' Perceptions of their needs and the Retailers' Marketing Strategies

In general, there is no significant difference between Omani and non-Omani customers ($p \geq 0.01$-$p \geq 0.05$) on most issues raised in terms of the customer needs and/or criteria, as well as perceptions of marketing strategies in Oman, such, as prices, brands, location convenience, perceived good value for money, availability of special products, quality of service and marketing strategies, as discussed below. However, some differences were found, see below. This could be related to cultural differences, as the study sample comprised different nationality and ethnic groups representing the multinational and multicultural context in Oman in general and Muscat region in particular. This is because Oman hosts around fifty four nationalities, according to the latest census (Ministry of National Economy, 2004).

A) Customers' Perception of the Importance of Low Prices

Omanis (88.17%) and non-Omanis (85.26%) equally perceived the importance of low prices in their shopping pattern and choice of hypermarket/supermarket, as they ranked this criterion as the most favourable one; Figure 4.1 and Appendix E: Table 4.1.

Omanis (89.79%) and non-Omanis (84.03%) ranked the importance of the *availability of different brands and prices variety* as one of the most important criteria; Figure 4.2, Appendix E: Table 4.2. This was also emphasised by the management and staff of LuLu that LuLu's competitive edge is, "Giving the customer the right of choice of different brands, qualities and prices of similar products because of LuLu's as low price has been perceived as the customer's most important criterion", Appendix C.

Figure 4.1: Customers' Perception of the Importance of Low Prices

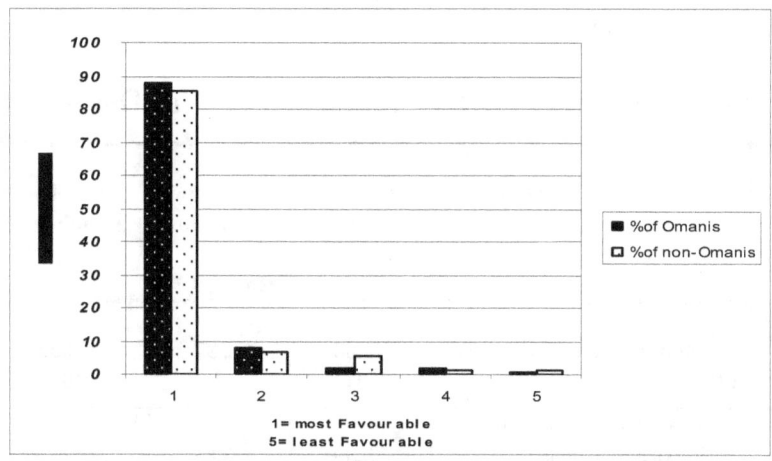

* Ranking scale: 1 = Most favourable; 2 = Favourable, 3 = Uncertain;
4 = Not favourable; 5 = Least favourable.

Entire Population: **838**	Degree of Freedom: **4**	Chi-Square (x^2) 9.50	$p = 0.05$

Figure 4.2: Customers' Perception of the Importance of Brands, quality and Prices Variety

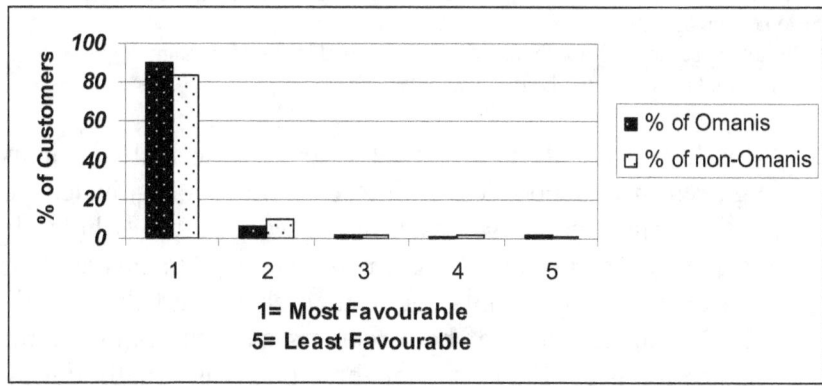

* Ranking scale: 1 = Most favourable; 2 = Favourable; 3 = Uncertain;
4 = Not favourable; 5 = Least favourable.

Entire Population: **838**	Degree of Freedom: **4**	Chi-Square (x^2) 7.62	$p < 0.25$ (0.106)

B) Customers' Perceptions of Different Types of Discounts

Table 4.2 outlines the discrepancy between the Omanis' and the non-Omanis' perceptions.

Table 4.2: Customers' Perceptions of Types of Discounts

No.*	Customers' Perception of Importance of Prices	Omanis % & Ranking**	Non-Omanis Perception & Ranking**	Level of Significance
4.3	Monthly discounts and special offers	92.58 (1)	72.97 (2)	x^2: 505.98 $p<0.01$
4.4	Seasonal discounts (e.g. return to school and Month of Ramadan)	78.89 (1)	48.89 (2)	x^2: 532.17 $p<0.01$
4.5	Discounted prices on certain products (e.g. Carrefour's Vendors', LuLu's clothes and electronics)	46.17 (3)	57.25 (3)	x^2: 124.79 $p<0.01$
4.6	Wholesale and family size products	92.11 (1)	27.27 (3)	x^2: 492.52 $p<0.01$

* It refers to numbers of tables and detailed results in Appendix E.
** The highest percentage and the corresponding ranking of the Omani and non-Omani customer perceptions.
*** Ranking scale: 1 = Most favourable; 2 = Favourable, 3 = Uncertain;
    4 = Not favourable; 5 = Least favourable.

1. 'Monthly discounts and special offers', 'seasonal discounts (e.g., return to school and Month of Ramadan [equivalent to the Christmas shopping season in the west])'; and 'wholesale and family size products' were perceived by Omanis as their most favourable discounts due to their shopping habits, Table 4.2. Managerial staff of both retailers gave the rationale for such preference, "Shopping for the Omanis is usually during the first 10 days of the month and during the Month of Ramadan". For this reason, profit or loss is usually decided by the success in attracting Omanis during these days or special seasons.

2. There was an agreement between the Omanis and non-Omanis in terms of 'discounted prices on certain products (e.g., Carrefour's vendors, LuLu's clothes and electronics)', as this criterion was ranked third on the scale, Table 4.2. In fact, this has been the survival marketing strategy for Carrefour to attract its customers due to its good network with different vendors and wholesalers of low cost goods such as garments. "Vendors are doing us (Carrefour) a great favour", a manager of Carrefour said.

C) *Customers' Perceptions of Raffles, Prizes and Earning Points*

Table 4.3: Omani and the Non-Omani Customers' Perceptions of Raffles, and Earning Points

No*.	Customers' Perception	Omanis % & Ranking**	Non-Omanis Perception & Ranking**	Level of Significance
4.7	Raffles and prizes (e.g., cars)	88.17% (1)	66.34% (1)	x^2: 63.14 $p<0.01$
4.8	Earning points and rewards card	78.89% (5)	40.54% (5)	x^2: 161.86 $p<0.01$

* It refers to numbers of tables and detailed results in Appendix E.
** The highest percentage and the corresponding ranking of the Omani and non-Omani customer perceptions.
*** Ranking scale: 1 = Most favourable; 2 = Favourable, 3 = Uncertain; 4 = Not favourable; 5 = Least favourable.

There were a general agreement between Omanis and non-Omanis in their perception of '*Raffles and prizes* (e.g., cars). They also agreed that LuLu offers the best prizes, 'Dream cars: 5 Mercedes E230 Cars' and '4 Four-Wheel Drive Cars', Table 4. Indeed, only LuLu can afford to offer such prizes due to its highest market share in Oman, and its strongest buyer's power when dealing with suppliers. At the meantime, LuLu maintains its low price policy; by watching and matching its competitors higher cost supplied products on daily basis, if not "more than one time during the day", as reported by managerial staff. In fact, Carrefour's staff also indicated, "We follow the same price watching policy," but LuLu maintains its competitive advantage and its buying and diversified buying power in 16 countries, where LuLu produces its own products.

'***Earning points and rewards card***s' was perceived as 'least favourable' by Omanis and non-Omanis. The different perception of the non-Omanis (40.54%) is due to cultural differences between the western minority and the majority of the Asian expatriates, Table 4.3. This could be disappointing to both global retailers who have the information technology capable of using the data provided by these cards to analyse customer shopping patterns. On the other hand, Sultan Centre uses this marketing strategy as it targets different niches, high income western customers as well as Omani and Arabic-speaking clients with western exposure

D) Customer Perceptions of the Importance of Special Products and Convenient Location

The discrepancy between Omani and non-Omani needs is clearly illustrated. The highest percentage of Omanis (only 28.31%) indicated that the '***importance of special product***s' is the least favourable, while non-Omanis (79.12%) ranked it the highest, Appendix E: Table 4.9. Accordingly, one can conclude that Omanis find the products they need in all hypermarkets and supermarkets. Both Carrefour and LuLu consider the Omanis as their marketing segment. The competitive edge of LuLu is targeting most of the niches of non-Omanis, e.g., LuLu imports fresh vegetables and fruits on a daily basis from these Indian and Asian expatriates' countries of origin and highlights special corners for products from different countries.

Actually there was no agreement within the groups of Omanis and non-Omnis in ranking the importance of '***convenient location***'. For example, the highest percentage of the Omanis (only 25.75%) ranked it third, while 32.43% of the non-Omanis perceived location as the least important criterion, Appendix E: Table 4.10.

That could be due the fact families have more than one car and the cost of a gallon of petrol is less than £0.7. It also seems that travelling time is not a decisive factor too.

E) Customers' Perception of the Importance of Quality of Service

Last but not least, Omanis (67.98%) and none Omanis (77.98%) ranked it as their most important criterion, Figure 4.3 and Appendix E: Table 4.11. Indeed, the quality of service, which cannot be copied or cloned, is the one which usually makes the difference, and provides a competitive edge to its provider.

Figure 4.3: Customers' Perception of the Importance of Quality of Service

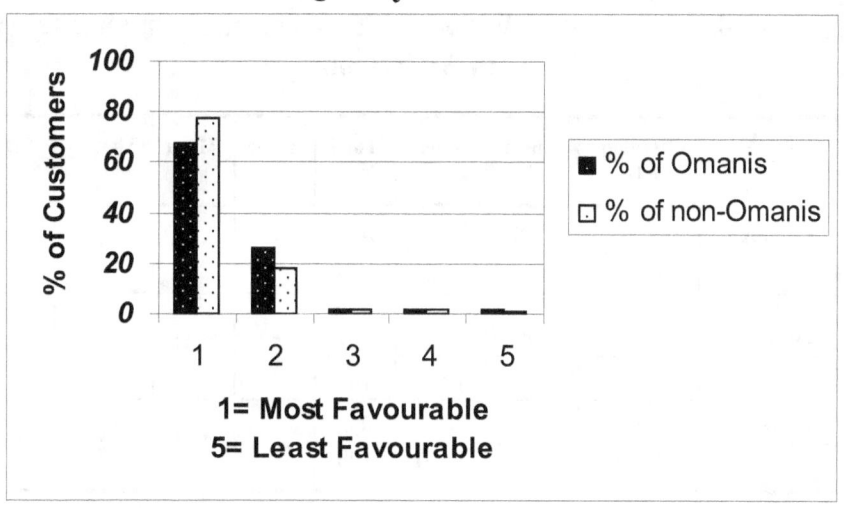

*** Ranking scale: 1 = Most favourable; 2 = Favourable, 3 = Uncertain;
    4 = Not favourable; 5 = Least favourable.

Entire Population: **838**	Degree of Freedom:	Chi-Square (x^2) **11.53**	$p<0.05$

Taking into account the above-mentioned results and analysis, the first hypothesis was partly rejected.

H.1	There is no significant difference between Omani and non-Omani customers in perceiving customers' needs and/or criteria, as well as their perceptions of marketing strategies in Oman, such as: a) Low prices as well as variety of brands, quality of products and prices b) Different types of discounts c) Raffles and prizes as well as earning points and reward cards d) Special products and convenient location e) Quality of service	*Partly Rejected*

IV. Reasons for Customers' Perceptions of LuLu as their Favourite Shopping Place and its Marketing Strategies

Table 4.4: Customers' Favourite Hypermarket/ Supermarket in All Regions

Scale Nationality	Carrefour 1	LuLu 2	Others 3	Total	Mode	Mean	Median	SD
Omani N	55	318	58	431	2	2.01	2	0.51
%	12.76	73.78	13.46	100				
Non-Omani N	63	272	72	407	2	2.02	2	0.58
%	15.48	66.83	17.69	100				
Total N	118	590	130	838	**2**	**2.01**	**2**	**0.54**
%	**14.08**	**70.41**	**15.51**	**100**				

Degree of Freedom: **3**	Chi-Square (x^2) 4.95	$p<0.10$ (0.084)

The majority, of the Omanis (73.78%) and the non-Omanis (66.83%) perceived **LuLu as their favourite shopping place**. On the other hand, only *14.08%* of the entire study sample perceived Carrefour, the *former market leader*, as their favourite hypermarket, Table 4.4.

The following findings provide the customers' rationale for the appreciation of LuLu's marketing strategies. Table 4.5 provides by the breakdown of the most attractive marketing strategies.

a) 65.20% of the Omanis and 71.99% of the non-Omanis perceived LuLu as offering *the best value for money*.
b) 64.97% of the Omanis and 70.76% of the non-Omanis perceived LuLu as offering *the best service*.
c) 69.37% of the Omanis and 68.55% of the non-Omanis perceive *LuLu as having the best products*.
d) 72.39% of the Omanis and 67.08% of the non-Omanis perceive *LuLu as having more special products* (e.g. from countries of origin & delicatessen).
e) 88.86% of the Omanis and 73.96% of the non-Omanis perceive *LuLu as offering the best raffles and prizes*.

Table 4.5: Summary of Omani and Non-Omani Customers' Perceptions of the Best Hypermarkets/Supermarkets (LuLu)

No.*	Customers' Perception	% of Omanis & their Choice**	% of Non-Omanis & their Choice**	Level of Significance
4.12	The best value for money	65.20 (LuLu)	71.99 (LuLu)	x^2: 5.32 $p<0.25$
4.13	The best service	64.97 (LuLu)	70.76 (LuLu)	x^2: 7.91 $p<0.050$
4.14	Having the best products	69.37 (LuLu)	68.55 (LuLu)	x^2: 4.72 $p<0.25$
4.15	Having special products (e.g. from countries of origin & delicatessen)	72.39 (LuLu)	67.08 (LuLu)	x^2: 28.98 $p<0.01$
4.16	Offering the best raffles and prizes	88.86 (LuLu)	73.96 (LuLu)	x^2: 48.87 $p<0.01$

* It refers to numbers of tables and detailed results in Appendix E.
** The highest percentage and the corresponding choice of the Omani and non-Omani customers' perception. According to the ranking scale: 1 = Carrefour, 2 = LuLu and 3 = other hypermarkets/supermarkets.

What provides LuLu with such a competitive advantage is that, "LuLu caters for the needs of the Omanis, the marketing segment and the different niches of the non Omanis. For example, LuLu imports fresh authentic vegetables and fruits daily and it provides different products from different countries to meet the needs of different ethnic groups, Arabs, Asians, Indians and westerners", as reported by LuLu's managers. Furthermore, LuLu provides a better quality of service than Carrefour's due to its staff satisfaction, positive attitude and team spirit, see Chapter 5. Accordingly, the second hypothesis was partly rejected.

H.2	There is no significant difference between the Omani and non-Omani customers in their perception of the marketing strategies, including the quality of products or the variety of brands and prices, as well as the quality of service provided by Carrefour and LuLu hypermarkets in Oman.	*Partly Rejected*

V.   *Customer Perceptions of Quality of Service*

Table 4.6 classifies the perceptions of Omani and non-Omani customers as to different aspects of customer service which depends mainly on the customer orientation of the staff, including personality trait of staff (Brown et al., 2002). Clearly, LuLu is favoured compared to Carrefour or other retailers.

Taking into account the Omanis and the non-Omani customers' perceptions of the quality of service, its availability and their frequency of using it when comparing LuLu's to Carrefour's or other competitors', the third hypothesis is partly rejected.

H.3	There is no significant difference between the perceptions of the Omani and non-Oman customers' perceptions in terms of the quality of services received as well as their availability in their favourite hypermarkets/supermarkets: Carrefour, LuLu or others.	*Partly Rejected*

Table 4.6: Summary of Quality of Service as Perceived by Omanis and the Non-Omanis in their favourite Hypermarkets/Supermarkets

No.	Customers' Perception	Carrefour Append. E: Tables 4.17-4.21 N=118	LuLu Append. E: Tables 4.22-4.26 N=590	Others Append. E: Tables 4.27-4.31 N=130
i	Using Services Omani Non-Omani	67.27% (3) 63.49% (3) (*p*<0.5)	91.19%(3) 84.56%(2)	81.03%(2) 50.00%(2)
ii	Availability of services Omani Non-Omani	52.73% (4) 69.84%(3)	84.91%(2) 83.82%(2) (*p*<0.5)	72.41%(2) 44.44%(2)
iii	Getting the expected service Omani Non-Omani	52.73% (4) 60.32%(3)	77.04%(2) 88.24%(2)	55.17%(2) 48.61%(3)
iv	Having your complaints taken seriously Omani Non-Omani	67.27% (1) 53.97% (3)	84.59%(2) 81.62%(1)	48.28%(2) 45.83%(3)
v	Receiving satisfactory solutions or help Omani Non-Omani	52.73% (2) 50.79% (3)	69.18%(1) 84.93%(1)	72.41%(2) 44.44%(2)

- N = the numbers who chose a particular hypermarket/supermarket as their 'favourite.' That is why the numbers vary.
- The highest percentage was chosen and the numbers between brackets describe the frequency: (1)=always; (2)=often; (3)=sometimes; (4)=Never.

VI. Summary and Conclusion

In response to the Customers' Questionnaire, there was no significant difference (p>0.01-p>0.05) between the Omani (N. 431) and the non-Omani (N. 407) study sample on most issues raised in terms of the customers' needs and/or criteria, as well as marketing strategies of Carrefour, LuLu and other retailers. These needs, criteria and marketing strategies included prices, brands, location convenience, favourite hypermarket/supermarket, perceived good value for money, availability of special products, quality of service, and their favourite hypermarket's/supermarket's marketing strategy. This was also emphasised in response to clients' ranking scale of the customers' identified needs and wants; their favourite hypermarket's/ supermarket's marketing strategy and its quality of service as illustrated above, Figures 4.1 and 4.3 Tables 4.2-4.6; Appendix E: Tables 4.1-4.31. On the other hand, the statistical analysis and the level of significance was between ($p<0.1$) and $p<0.5$) when measuring the Omanis' and the non-Omanis' perception' of the overall quality of service by Carrefour's and LuLu's hypermarkets as listed below:

   a) "Importance of variety of brands and prices", Figure 4.2; Appendix E, Table 4.2, ($p<0.25$).
   b) Table 4.4: "Perceiving LuLu as their favourite supermarket in all regions", ($p<0.1$)
   c) "Perceiving LuLu as offering the best value for money", Table 4.5; Appendix E, Tables 4.12, ($p<0.25$).
   d) "Perceiving LuLu as offering the best products", ($p<0.25$), Table 4.5; Appendix, E, Table 4.14.
   e) "Customers' frequency of using Carrefour's services", Table 4.6; Appendix E, Table; 4.17, ($p<0.5$).
   f) "Customers' perception of the availability of LuLu's services", Table 4.6; Appendix E, Tables; 4.23, ($p<0.5$).

The rationale for such differences is due to the customers' different cultural backgrounds and consequently their needs and perceptions of the different marketing strategies adopted by Carrefour, LuLu and other retailers. Such differences are found not only between the large diversity of the non-Omani population, but also between the Omanis due to their exposure or even immersion in other cultures, such as Zanzibar, which used to be ruled by Oman. Briefly, due to the cultural awareness of these needs, LuLu's management succeeded to meet such needs and tailor its marketing strategies as well as its recruitment policies to address the general Omani segment as well as most of the niches of the non-Omani.

Briefly, most of the customers expressed their overall satisfaction with LuLu's different elements including ***Product***, ***Pricing***,

Promotion, *Place* ("convenient place" was perceived as the least important), and its quality and availability of service compared to Carrefour and other retailers. In so doing, hypotheses 1-3 were partly rejected.

In conclusion, Carrefour lost its role as a market leader to LuLu, as the latter's business strategy caters for meeting the multicultural and multi ethnic groups of the Omani population and most of the non-Omani niches in most regions of the country. For example:

a) LuLu has adopted an aggressive expansion strategy (TheWeek, 2008; Oman Tribune, 2008). It has been opening and acquiring many supermarkets/ hypermarkets all over Oman starting in Muscat and the areas of highest density of the Omani population. Accordingly, LuLu opts for the market shares of global and local retailer in Oman, Table 6.1.

b) Most of the Omani and non-Omani customers perceived LuLu as their favourite hypermarket/supermarket for many reasons.

c) No doubt LuLu has acquired a competitive advantage against its competitors in the form of having a buying power with its suppliers resulting in lower costs (Hunt and Morgan, 1996).

d) So, LuLu could offer raffles of 5 Mercedes 'dream cars' on one occasion, which other hypermarkets cannot afford to do so. Such an incentive or promotion was also ranked as one of the most important criteria of most Omani and non-Omani customers.

e) LuLu also succeeded in copying and adapting the marketing strategies of Carrefour, Nestlé and Unilever.

f) What has distinguished LuLu compared to Carrefour and other retailers is its immediate response to its customers' needs and MO.

g) Customers also perceived LuLu's quality of service as the best, compared to other retailers and indicated that distance and time are not of importance for them. LuLu's quality of service takes also into account the after sale service.

h) Indeed, LuLu's asset is its satisfied and secured staff which is characterised by its team spirit, loyalty and commitment, Chapter 5, due to the organisation culture and LuLu's business philosophy, Chapter 6.

Data Analysis and Results II:
5   Staff Perception of the Organisation, Cultural Diversity and Level of Satisfaction

I. Introduction and Background of Case Study II

Chapter 4 reviewed and analysed data collected from 838 multinational and multicultural customers, Omanis and non-Omanis. In so doing, these customers' perceptions of their needs and wants were examined, as well as the marketing strategies of both Carrefour (MAF Group) and LuLu (EMKE Group), with the aim of identifying their weaknesses and strengths. The study has clearly indicated the higher level of satisfaction of both Omani and non-Omani customers with the latter's marketing strategies.

To measure individual perception of organisation culture, employees' attitude and level of satisfaction, this study used "Staff Questionnaire", Appendix B, which ranked organisational and individual culture 5-point scale: 5 = strongly disagree to 1 = strongly agree, for the first 20 questions of 22 questions. Questions 1-8 aimed at identifying how the employees perceived the actual situation, or organisational culture of the respective firm, Carrefour or LuLu.

Questions 9-16 aimed to measure to what extent employees were satisfied with the present situation or organisational culture. Questions 17-20 identified the staff's attitude towards their respective firms. Questions 21-23 aimed at collecting personal data. Questions 25-26 were open-ended questions requesting further information and suggestions. The study sample comprised 53 of Carrefour's mangers and staff and 60 of LuLu's. During the interviews, managers and staff in the two *centralised firms* insisted on not mentioning their names, their posts and in some cases the branch's name. Therefore, it was agreed to use general terms such as staff and managers in order to keep the identity of the respondents confidential. The study aimed at:

a) Measuring the person-environment fit and the organisation-environment fit in the Omani market and the effects on the corporate business strategy in Oman. Most of the 'Staff Questionnaire: Business Cultural Values' were completed in the staff residences through a few of the staff whose trust the writer succeeded to gain. The twenty-two filled questionnaires by the Omani staff were discretely administered in Arabic on the retailer's premises. Ten incomplete questionnaires were excluded to avoid any statistical bias.

b) Gaining access to general managers, managers, assistant managers and even staff, particularly when required to to answer the questions of the 'Semi-Structured Interviews for Global Retailers and Suppliers', Appendix C, was not easy, for organisational policies and cultural reasons. Therefore, the analysis takes into account the data collected by using semi-structured interviews, which comprised 33 open-ended questions. The respondents of these interviews were top and middle managers of Carrefour (6) and LuLu (15) as well as two of each of their suppliers of global products, i.e. Nestlé, Unilever, Sony, Canon, and HP located in Muscat, Oman. Accordingly, the interviews *discretely* took place on the retailers' premises.

II   *Individual's Perception of Organisation Culture in a Multinational Context*

Table 5.1 outlines the discrepancy between the responses of Carrefour and LuLu staff. However, the issues where there seemed to be an agreement between the staff of both firms are discussed below:

a) Bearing in mind that the employees of the two retailers belongs to 'power-distance' and 'uncertainty/avoidance' groups (Hofstede, 1980), 84.91% of Carrefour's and 75% of LuLu's negatively perceived 'Daily Written reports'. This is because reports are perceived by most Arabic and Asians cultures as documents which can be misused by those in authority.

Table 5.1: Carrefour's and LuLu's Staff Perception of the Actual Situation and their Level of Satisfaction

No*.	Staff's Perception	Actual Situation Versus Level of Satisfaction	Carrefour's Staff % & Ranking**		LuLu's Staff % & Ranking**		x^2 Level of Sign.	t-test Level of Sign.
			%	Rank	%	Rank		
5.1		Actual	75.47	4	76.67	2	p<0.001	p<0.001
5.2	Job descriptions	Satisfaction	56.60	4	70.00	2	p<0.001	p<0.001
5.3		Actual	73.58	4	78.33	2	p<0.001	p<0.001
5.4	Clear rules	Satisfaction	71.70	4	66.67	2	p<0.001	p<0.001
5.5	Daily Written	Actual	84.91	5	75.00	4	p<0.001	p<0.001
5.6	reports	Satisfaction	75.47	4	75.00	2	p<0.001	p<0.001
5.7	Communicate	Actual	77.36	3	88.33	3	*p<0.25*	P<0.05
5.8	through formal channels	Satisfaction	62.26	4	70.00	2	p<0.001	p<0.001
5.9	Have say in	Actual	84.91	4	75.00	2	p<0.001	p<0.001
5.10	decisions	Satisfaction	84.91	4	63.33	2	p<0.001	p<0.001
5.11	Free to	Actual	73.58	4	63.33	2	p<0.001	p<0.001
5.12	communicate upward & downward.	Satisfaction	73.58	4	68.33	2	p<0.001	p<0.001
5.13	Access to Data	Actual	75.47	4	75.00	2	p<0.001	p<0.001
5.14	and information	Satisfaction	75.47	4	75.00	2	p<0.001	p<0.001
5.15	Direct	Actual	81.13	4	63.33	4	*p<0.25*	*p>0.20*
5.16	feedback and criticism to superiors	Satisfaction	69.81	4	66.67	4	*p<0.5*	*p<0.5*

* Number of Tables in Appendix F.
** The highest percentage and the corresponding ranking of Carrefour's and LuLu's staff perception and level of satisfaction was expressed as follows: 5 = Strongly disagree, 4 = Agree, 3 = Neutral, 2 = Disagree, and 1 = Strongly agree.

b) 77.36% of Carrefour's staff and 88.33% of Lulu's chose to be 'neutral' when they were requested to describe the actual situation: 'Communicate through formal channels'. This is also related to their cultural background in relation to work related values. However, 70% of LuLu's employees agreed with the idea of communicating through formal channels.

c) 77.36% of Carrefour's and 88.33% of Lulu's employees disagreed with the statement: 'direct feedback and criticism to superiors' in describing the 'actual situation'. Furthermore, 69.81% of Carrefour's and 66.67% of LuLu's chose to be 'neutral' when they were asked to respond to the same statement describing their level of satisfaction. Hofstede's classification of work related values 'power-distance' and 'uncertainty/ avoidance' rightly describes this context. However, most of LuLu's employees expressed their high level of satisfaction, team spirit, commitment and loyalties, as in the oriental 'patriarchal' system, individuals are not expected to criticise their superiors or the elders.

As the responses from Carrefour and Lulu's staff differed for most statements, the fourth hypothesis is partly rejected.

H. 4	There is no significant difference between the organisation culture and the style of management of both the Global retailers in Oman, i.e., Carrefour and LuLu Hypermarkets, as perceived by their respective staff.	Partly Rejected

III. Staff Attitude towards the Organisational Environment *in a Multinational Context*

The statistical analysis, Pearson's Chi Square and the t-*test*, of the respondents' responses were significant at $p<0.001$ in all statements, except 'Having pride in their company'. In fact, 75.47% of Carrefour's staff and 70% of LuLu's agreed with the statement. On the other hand, Carrefour's staff agreement flatly contradicts their earlier and coming responses. Such contradictory positive perception could be due to two reasons, which are Carrefour's staff is generally paid higher than other retailers, including LuLu's, and the fact that Carrefour is still perceived as a franchised French company, Table 5.2.

LuLu managers and employees reported that, "We are a family". They added that they work as a team in a "secured business environment". On the other hand, most of Carrefour staff felt 'insecure' and some were being 'harassed', e.g., one of the remaining Indian managerial staff said, "Carrefour was built on our shoulders, and we are being harassed." He also added that "the non-Omani Arabic-speakers' monthly salary is fifty Omani Riyals higher than the others (Indians)".

Another manager said, "The Head Office in Dubai (decision makers in a centralised organisation) is controlled by Lebanese nationals". A Jordanian head of department stated that, "I keep records and photos of my department shelves, as evidence of my good work, to be able to defend myself when I am unfairly reported or blamed."

Perhaps, Lebanese are perceived by the MAF Group as having an advantage in being bilingual, Arabic and French. Although this might be true in relation to the senior managerial staff when communicating with the French Carrefour Head Office in Paris, but not with marketing staff dealing with customers in Oman, where Arabic and English are the medium of communication. When the writer quoted these statements to a senior managerial non-Arab staff, his answer was brief, "I am implementing a company policy". Furthermore, I overheard a French manager being told, "Carrefour is an Arab company, not a French one, as it is owned by the UAE national, Majid Al Futtaim."

LuLu also adopts unequal pay policy, as only Omani staff is given a monthly twenty five Riyals as an incentive if he/she does not miss a working day for medical or any other reasons. A managerial staff said, "A junior Omani's monthly salary ends higher than mine". LuLu unequal pay policy may be justified as favouring Omanis in their own country. These are a few examples to illustrate how organisation culture is different in global companies' countries. If Carrefour and LuLu discriminate against the employees in non-Gulf countries, they would be legally challenged.

Table 5.2: Carrefour's and LuLu's Staff Attitude Towards the Organisational Environment

Append. Tables & Graphs No.*	Staff's Attitude	Carrefour's Staff % & Ranking**		LuLu's Staff % & Ranking**		x^2 Level of Sign.	t-test Level of Sign
		%	Rank	%	Rank		
5.17	Presenting their company as a great place to work in	79.25	3	75.00	2	*p*<0.001	*p*<0.001
5.18	Having pride in their company	75.47	2	75.00	2	***p*<0.995**	***p*>0.20**
5.19	Company provides inspiration	75.47	4	78.33	2	*p*<0.001	*p*<0.001
5.20	Caring about the interest of the company	56.6	3	75.00	2	*p*<0.001	*p*<0.001

* Number of Tables in Appendix F.

** The highest percentage and the corresponding ranking of Carrefour's and LuLu's staff attitude and perception was expressed as follows: 5 = Strongly disagree, 4 = Agree, 3 = Neutral, 2 = Disagree, and 1 = Strongly agree.

Briefly, most of the responses of Carrefour's staff were different from LuLu's. Accordingly, the fifth hypothesis has been partly rejected.

H. 5	There is no significant difference between the staff's *level of satisfaction* of Carrefour and LuLu Hypermarkets' with their organisation culture and the style of management.	Partly Rejected

V. Intangible Resources: Recruitment, Training and Company's Performance

Table 5.3 classifies the total number of staff Carrefour and LuLu employed in all branches in Oman (Ministry of Manpower database on 12th May 2008). Tables 3.2-3.4 also classify the staff study sample by nationality, level of education and training as well as by job level. Table 5.3 also shows the number and percentage of Omani employees of Carrefour (54.55%). Omani employees comprise graduates of Omani secondary schools who received their pre-job training from an Omani private institute 'Al Rakaeb'. LuLu's Omani staff (36.45%) received their pre-job training from the 'Polyglot Institute'. In fact, such training is the Ministry of Manpower's requirement, which employers have to provide to new staff. On the other hand, the quality and the relevance of such training need to be evaluated, as this is beyond the scope of this volume.

Table 5.3: Numbers of Omani and Non-Omani Employees of Carrefour and LuLu

Retailer		Omani Staff*			Non-Omani Staff			Grand Total		
		M	F	Total	M	F	Total	M	F	Total
Carrefour	N	272	52	324	231	39	270	503	91	594
	%	83.95	16.05	100	85.56	14.44	100	84.68	15.32	100
LuLu	N	422	530	952	1621	39**	1660	2043	569	2612
	%	44.33	55.67	100	97.65	2.35	100	78.22	21.78	100
Grand Total	N	694	582	1276	1852	78	1930	2546	660	3206
	%	54.39	45.61	100	95.96	4.04	100	79.41	23.70	100

* 54.55% Omanis are working in Carrefour, while 36.45% Omanis are working for LuLu.
** Mainly from Philippines, as they are perceived as more hygienic.

One may also bear in mind that only 15.48% of the 838 customer study sample perceived Carrefour as their favourite retailer, while 66.83% perceived LuLu, Table 4.4. Furthermore, only 14.08% of the customer sample perceived Carrefour as offering *the best service*, while 70.41% perceived LuLu, Table 4.5.   Indeed, the implications of these findings require further investigation.

  a) Has the induction of Carrefour's Omani employees made a difference, bearing in mind that Carrefour's staff is pre-trained by a local training institute, while Lulu's is pre-trained by a global one, through the medium of English?
  b) Is the gender proportion a factor that has influenced the provided quality of service, 15.32% of Carrefour's staff is female, while 21.78% of LuLu's?
  c) Have the recruitment policies and the organisational culture influenced the attitude of the employees?
     Unfortunately, the answer to these questions is beyond the scope of this study.

Recruitment, Selection Assessment, Training and Appraisal

a) Carrefour

The high turnover of the employees can be related to organisational culture reasons mentioned above. It should also be noted some of the senior managerial staff had experience with other retailers, like Spinneys.   The Human resources (HR) Manager in Oman is Indian. He has to deal with the Ministry of Manpower through an Omani HR officer. In fact, the Ministry of Manpower is the one nominating new Omani staff for recruitment. Training takes different forms, mainly shadowing, workshops and newsletters. Appraisal is done in a formal manner and is theoretically discussed with the concerned employee and signed by both the assessor and the appraised. Promotions and awards were reported to be "organisational goals."

b) LuLu

LuLu recruits the non-Omani applicants in Oman through a committee which comprises the General Manager and the Human Resources Manager of Baushar Branch in Muscat, as well the General Manager of the respective Branch.

It was reported that Indian style of management has been "influenced by the British rule, its style of management and gained experience". However, there are some *'cultural differences'* between Indian and western styles of management. For example, "Indian employees are driven by their cultural value of being 'duty' bound (*Krama*)". For Indians work is viewed as an extension of their personal lives. Therefore, Indian organisations have a wide range of recruitment and HR management strategies which are fairly informal when compared to British or western strategies. On the other hand, Carrefour style of management aims at meeting global standards of management strategies.

Most of the recruitment of LuLu Indian employees is done on humanitarian basis. A manager said, "God is the provider ... God's gifts are forwarded to the needy through LuLu." For example, Mr. Youssiali, the CEO, sits on the board of different orphanages in India, where he recruits a high percentage of LuLu's staff. He employs only one member, usually a male, of the families in remote poor areas of India, to work at LuLu and be the family bread-winner. These staff members need no pre-requisites. Training is done by LuLu's managers and senior staff, mostly MBA holders, but paid around than £300 a month (Ministry of Manpower database, 12th May 2008). The following statements were heard from more than one employee:

a) "Indian culture encourages sharing knowledge, so, we share knowledge and experience on site"

b) "Managers take time to train other employees, thus propagating knowledge within LuLu"

c) "Our (LuLu/Indians) concept of monitoring is slightly different from western style, where it is more formal and budgeted, while for us (LuLu/Indians) it is informal and not budgeted"

d) "Managers are accountable for learning, instead of results"

Furthermore, it was emphasised and observed that "LuLu's employees are employed for life and from different ethnic groups and religions." Managers are usually attracted from global companies in India, such as Marriot Hotel. Such selection is done

by the CEO. In this context, several phrases were repeated including:
a) "Employees are LuLu's great asset"
b) "Staff retention is LuLu's policy"
c) "What is important to LuLu and its employees is to figure a way to 'marry' them, so they feel an integral part of LuLu and understand their contribution and value"
d) "Three marketers left LuLu for a better pay offered by a competitor, but returned back for our family atmosphere (organisation culture)". It happened to meet them by accident earlier.

However, some of LuLu's non-Indian (Asian) staff left after completing their first contract due to some frustration. One of them reported, "I am leaving at the end of the contract as I am an accountant, and wishes to work as an accountant (not a salesperson)". On the other hand, many of her Indian colleagues are MBA holders, and satisfied doing their job. That could be due to their sense of job security, loyalty and commitment. Promotions and rewards are reported to be according to performance, commitment and loyalty. A few Omanis with strong or 'forceful' personality are also given some senior positions, but to:

> "Ensure Omani employees follow rules, and to avoid confrontation between Omani staff and (non-Omani) management or Ministry of Manpower."

Accordingly, the last hypothesis was partly rejected.

H.6.	There is no significant difference between policies when dealing with 'intangible' resources, such as human resources and their training as well as recruitment in global companies' countries of origin, and in the host countries.	Partly Rejected

V. Conclusion

Indeed, organisation culture has influenced the perception of the actual situation and the level of satisfaction and attitude of the employees of Carrefour and LuLu in Oman. The responses to the 'Staff Questionnaire', Appendix B, and the data analysis were mostly positive by LuLu's staff, unlike Carrefour's. This might have positive implications in relation to the marketing and the financial performance of LuLu. LuLu also benefited from the ethnic and cultural diversity of its staff as well as staff commitment due to job security, while Carrefour's employees suffer from job insecurity.

The responses to the semi-structured interviews and the observations indicated that global producers (e.g., Carrefour) or suppliers generally provide products according to the different regions of the world in terms of flavour or taste, size of package and specifications, where applicable, but not for a particular country like Oman. On the other hand, LuLu caters in many of its products in sixteen Asian and African countries for its large size family Omani customers, in addition to importing daily authentic products for the different ethnic Indian and Asian niches. In terms of research and development, this depends of the producer and the market needs, e.g., LuLu was fast in responding to the Omni Market needs and the sudden rise of groceries and other products, while Carrefour in Oman, UAE or in France did not respond to the Omani market needs.

6 Summary, Implications and Conclusions

I. Key Points

Based on the empirical findings, the study focused on market orientation (MO), which is considered "… a cornerstone of marketing and management strategy" (Gray and Hooley, 2002, p. 980). In so doing, this MO analysis includes similarities (e.g., strong focus on customers, external orientation, being responsive to customers, and focus on more than customers), as well as differences, e.g., behavioural versus cultural perspective and differences in terms used, i.e., market oriented, market driven and customer oriented, (Jaworski and Kohli, 1993). Furthermore, the study examined the impact of cultural diversity and global management on person-environment fit as well as marketing strategies. It demonstrates challenges that the policy makers face in relation to not only marketing strategies, but also policies and procedures/styles of management, leadership, recruitment, training, innovation and use of information technology.

The qualitative and quantitative analyses also took into account MO which has been conceptualised as organisational behaviour, managerial choice (Jaworski and Kohli, 1993; Kohli and Jaworski, 1990; Ruekert, 1992), and organisational culture (Deshpandé, Farley, and Webster, 1993; Homburg and Pflesser, 2000; Narver and Slater, 1990; Slater and Narver, 1994). Accordingly, the key points are:

1) Carrefour (Majid Al Futtaim Group) has lost its role as a market leader to LuLu (EMKE Group), Appendix D, in Oman and probably in other Gulf countries, Figure 2.1.

Table 6.1: LuLu's Competitors and Threats
in the Different Regions in Oman

Regions	Threats/Competitors: The Major Clustered/Nearest Hypermarkets/ Supermarkets and Remarks
Muscat Area	
1 **Mattrah, Darsait, Ruwi**	**LuLu** (Darsait), **El Osra Supermarket**, Ruwi, and **Al Fair Supermarket** (Formerly Spinneys), Ruwi.
2 **Al Quorum, Al Sarouj, Al Ealaam**	**LuLu** (Baushar), **Sultan Centre** (Al Quorum), **Al Fair Supermarket** (Madinat Qaboos), (Al Quorum), **Al Fair** (Al Sarouj) **Al Fair Supermarket** (Khuwair, *closed down following the opening of LuLu*) and **Carrefour Hypermarket** (*Al Quorum opened at a later date*)
3 **North & South Ghubra, Ghala, Al Azaiba and Al Khuwair**	**LuLu Hypermarket** (Baushar), **Al Safeer Hypermarket** (The main Branch) and **Pick and Save Supermarket** (Al Safeer).
4 **Al Hail and Al Seeb**	**Carrefour** (Seeb), **Al Jumlah Hypermarket** (opened following the opening of Carrefour in Seeb, a branch of Sultan Centre), Then, **Al Burge Supermarket** (acquired recently by **LuLu** in Seeb). **Both are close to Carrefour.**
Al Batinah Region (The highest density of the Omani population)	
5 **North and South Al Mubeela, and Barka**	**LuLu Hypermarket** (Barka), **Al Tayeb Supermarket**, **Al Baraka Supermarket**. The population is mainly Omanis and a very low percentage of expatriates.
Salalah (Dhofar)	
6 **Salalah**	Al Istiqrar, Al Mashour as well as other small supermarkets

2) LuLu's business strategy is based on addressing Omani and non-Omani customer's needs and aggressive expansion, not only in all regions in Muscat, but also in the areas of highest density of the Omani population, competing with global retailers such as Carrefour, Al Fair (Formerly Spinneys), the Kuwaiti Sultan Centre, the North Indian Al Safeer as well as the local retailers such Al Tayeb, Al Baraka, Al Isteqrar, Table 6.1.

3) Having western clients is perceived by non-western customers in the Gulf as a certificate of quality. LuLu is playing well on this string which has been mastered by its CEO, Mr. Yusufali.

4) Maximizing the benefits of his close and personal relationship with the vegetables and fruits wholesalers in Oman and UAE who are also Keralite, providing LuLu with a strong network.

5) In fact, LuLu's CEO, Mr. Yusufali, is well connected not only to the top Indian leaders and politicians, but also to the rulers and the decision makers in the Gulf countries. He meets them regularly and has received many awards from Gulf rulers and the Indian government.

6) Importing fresh vegetables and fruits as well as some other fresh products on daily basis is a policy to meet the needs of different niches of LuLu's Indian and Asian clients.

7) The acquisition of "Al Borg Supermarket", the nearest supermarket to Carrefour, without changing its name, to maintain having its main segment of Omanis who came back from Zanzibar with their special taste and needs. In so doing, LuLu addresses not only the different cultural backgrounds of the non-Omanis, but also the Omanis.

8) Diversity of its staff from 16 countries that belong to different religions and ethnic groups to make the multicultural Omani and non-Omani feel welcome in its hypermarkets.

9) The high level of LuLu staff satisfaction, team spirit and life-long employment, unlike the unsatisfied and unsecured Carrefour's employees in Oman, Chapter 5.

Strengths of LuLu are summarised as follows:

1) LuLu's corporate philosophy is reinforced by its CEO, Mr. Yusufali: "Being faithful to its 'global localization' philosophy", which allowed the organisation-environment fit. On the other hand, the Franchised Carrefour failed to adapt to Omani market needs (Verdin, and van Heck, 2001).

2) LuLu has been gaining, due to its marketing approaches, by copying and adapting marketing strategies, such as Carrefour's, to meet the cultural diversity in the Omani market. In so doing, LuLu has succeeded in differentiating itself from its global and local competitors.

3) Being the fastest in responding to these needs and market MO, particularly following the sudden rise of food products and inflation rate.

4) In addition to addressing the needs of the main segment, the Omanis, LuLu also caters for the needs of other niches, e.g., the North Indians, Al Safeer's largest niche.

5) Being the largest retailer in the country, if not the entire Gulf, resulted in LuLu enjoying a good bargaining power with suppliers.

6) Providing many luxurious incentives to his customers, e.g. 5 Mercedes cars on offered as a raffle prize one occasion to attract customers.

7) Having its own factories in 16 countries in Asia and Africa and buying global brand's packed in its original suppliers' names, but discretely adding LuLu's logo on the pack, Nestlé's (acquiring) strategy.

8) Addressing the western niche needs by having a regular special corner of British products during Christmas and New Year as well as Easter. LuLu highlights the British products, which are perceived as a symbol of quality by Omanis and non-Omanis, by flying the British flag and having a replica of London Bridge in its stores. Furthermore, during the Christmas celebration in 2006, H.E. the British ambassador residence received mince pies, complements of LuLu Hypermarkets. In so doing, LuLu succeeded to attract most of Carrefour's, Al Fair's and Sultan Centre's main niches.

9) Copying Carrefour marketing strategies such as the promotion leaflets, seasonal promotions, and lowering the prices of fruits and vegetables. In addition, LuLu is also monitoring the other

local retailers copying Carrefour. In so doing, LuLu is combining both local and global strategies, which can be considered as a kind of innovation.

10) According to LuLu's CEO, "Innovation requires more than the processing of existing data. It requires human thought, teamwork, spontaneous intuition (and the Indian experience, connection and insights in the Gulf, including Oman), and a lot of courage we (LuLu) have".

11) Attracting its managerial staff from international organisations, mainly in India and the Gulf who are not well paid by international standards, who are usually able to train staff according to global companies' standards. This combines quality and lower cost, which is a competitive advantage.

12) Diversity of staff from sixteen countries is "LuLu's asset", in their managers' words, which helps to attract different niches of customers. This is typically used by firms, such as travel agencies, in the Gulf, e.g. Bahrain and Oman.

13) LuLu's recruitment policy, training and organisation culture results in loyalty and commitment and less costly, unlike Carrefour's.

Weaknesses of LuLu can be summarised as follows:

1) Centralised management, the head office is in Abu Dhabi, UAE; similar to Carrefour's, in Dubai, UAE.

2) Not located in large and entertaining shopping malls as Carrefour Hypermarket. This issue is being addressed by LuLu now, as it is expanding its present premises and renting spaces/shops to global, regional and local stores and restaurants.

3) LuLu hypermarket is on two levels; accordingly customers usually visit the food section only. The latest LuLu hypermarket in Barka is similar to Carrefour, as all departments are in one level, encouraging customers to visit all departments.

4) Not having a global brand name compared to Carrefour, the second large global retailer after Wal-Mart.

5) Having to recruit many inexperienced Omani staff and placing them in the front line, where they have to deal with customers,

such as cashiers, security guards, which is the same problem facing all retailers Oman.

6) Threat from new Global retailers, e.g. El Nakheel, which is coming forcefully to the Gulf, as the Gulf market seems attractive (Galal, 2008).

7) Neither Carrefour nor LuLu benefits from the available information technology facilities and staff, as they do not have a system which studies the customer shopping pattern, unlike Sultan Centre in Oman.

II. Implications for Policy and Practice

The results of this study can be beneficial for practitioners and enterprises in that it offers them managerial insights related to the research topic.   Some important implications for policy and practices are specially worth noting.

First, the findings were consistent with those of prior research that argued that the success of managerial practices and organisational design are dependent on an appropriate fit between the assumptions, values and beliefs inherent in the managerial practices in question and the culturally based assumptions, values and beliefs held by those who are being managed (Kikrman and Shapiro, 1997; Robert et al. 2000). Even within the same firm, employees at different sites or branches or similar firms in the same sector and in different job functions may demonstrate patterns of P-E fit that best fit their cultural values and making sense. Therefore, it is recommended that management theories and techniques developed in one cultural context, e.g., France or the USA may not be adequate in other cultural settings. Consequently, managers should be more sensitive and flexible in designing organisational culture. In so doing, local knowledge (either national culture or specific job functions) should be highly valued, and management policy should be locally adapted whenever possible. In other words, balancing local demands and global vision for a multinational enterprise is valid and pertinent (Ferraro, 1990; Prahalad and Doz, 1987).

The example of these functions (e.g., production, marketing and human resources), LuLu's employees generally showed higher commitment to their group when their values and commitment are close to those of their group. Therefore, managers may pay attention to recruiting and retaining people who hold similar values to the group as to keep certain degree of group homogeneity in these functions of being a market leader. Recruiting experienced mangers in multinational organisations that are distinctive and with higher commitment is a different policy of recruitment and management. Therefore, a different policy of recruitment and management, as it is the case in LuLu, should be applied to personnel in these two functions so as to maintain a higher degree of heterogeneity and to guarantee the flexibility that allows these employees to be 'different'. Higher commitment and maybe also improved creativity and innovative ideas, may be also the fruit of this flexible management practice.

Second, the results of this P-E fit and marketing study indicate how managers can improve their organisational design. The results indicated a common tendency, in LuLu, that higher satisfaction, commitment often occurred when the structure was perceived as highly formalised, appreciative and caring of its employees. Moreover, as mention in the study analysis of the two case studies, employees of all cultures considered the organisation to be structured in ways less formalised and less decentralised than their preference. Therefore, managers can consider how to increase the degree of formalisation and decentralisation in terms of internal communication style as to enhance the effectiveness of organisational design.

While the advantages of decentralisation may be obvious, the benefit of higher formalisation may be less intuitive. Therefore, managers should be able to distinguish 'enabling' from 'coercive' formalisation (Alder and Borys, 1996), and they should try to develop the former in their organisation. As Rousseau and Fried (2001) noted, while flexibility may be appreciated by employees, formal and clear rules of the game are also needed for the smooth functioning of the organisation. It is why enabling g formalisation is often desired and also why formalisation is usually perceived as not enough in organisations. Better organisational design can be achieved through the recognition of the importance of enabling formalisation and decentralisation by the managers and through their capability and will to put them into practice.

Thirdly, earlier research has indicated that MO increases a firm's performance (Jaworski and Kholi, 1993; Narver and Slater, 1990). Therefore, firms with employees who possess individual values/personality traits and attitudes that do not support MO may find themselves in a position of competitive disadvantage relative to other companies with more market-oriented staff.

Fourthly, other studies show that at the employee-level, individual values and personality traits influence individual attitudes towards MO. These attitudes then influence P-E fit and market-oriented behaviours. In this framework, values might be difficult to change because they are central to an individual's belief system and transcend specific situation (Rokeach, 1973). On the other hand, attitudes are easier to change, as they are less global in their application (Ajzen and Fishbein, 1980). In addition, behaviours are malleable and relatively easy to change. Furthermore, it has been argued in literature that behaviours also reinforce an individual's values and attitudes through a feedback effect (Day, 2003; Hartline et al., 2000; Meglino and Ravlin, 1998).

Thus, a manager wants to enhance his/her company's MO is expected to act in three different ways simultaneously (Schneider, White and Paul, 1998; Schneider and White, 2004). Each way reciprocally reinforces the other two.

1) A manager can select employees who possess favourable MO attitudes, based on their individual value and personality trait profiles. As it is difficult to change an individual value and personality, it is therefore easier to employ personnel who have values and personality traits that are consistent with the firm's desired MO oriented behaviours.

2) To reinforce employee favourable attitude towards MO, managers may develop MO training programmes/workshops aiming at making employees aware of cultural awareness, P-E fit and MO and their impact on individual performance and consequently on organisation performance. To be effective, these programmes should aim at changing employee attitude,

more than their values. Change comes about through altering behavioural models and by helping employees to understand how new behaviours may lead to improved performance, i.e. by changing attitude.

3) Managers are expected to develop incentive systems to reward employee market-oriented behaviours (Jaworski and Kholi, 1993). Eventually, these changes will be absorbed into employee value systems and attitudes.

4) Finally, in order to crystallise changes in attitudes and behaviours towards MO, it could be important to develop customer relationship management tools which would help individual employees to better serve the customers, obtain information about competitors and communicate more freely with other departments or managerial levels.

III. Research Implications and Conclusions

The value, personality or attitude, behaviour hierarchy works in the context of MO. Therefore, future MO research should not only focus on the company level, but also on the individual employee level, by taking into account the employee's personality and values, as well as their attitudes in order to better understand the relationship between market-oriented behaviour and individual performance. In so doing, personality in the value -attitude- behaviour hierarchy is to be examined (Fishbein and Ajzen, 1975).

Studies by Bettencourt, Gwinner and Meuter (2001), Bettencourt and Brown (2003), Bettencourt, Brown and MacKenzie (2005) and Brown et al. (2002) have focused their work on customer-contact employees. The results of these studies showed that even back-office staff should also be taken into account in order to better understand the link between market-oriented behaviour and individual performance in services companies.

Most research, within the culturally oriented perspective on MO, has taken contingency approach (Deshpandé and Webster, 1989; Usunier, 1996), by asking managers about their perceptions of their companies' MO. Further research is then recommended to identify similarities and differences among individual employees' values as well as personality traits, attitudes, behaviours, in order to study the diffusion of MO throughout the organisation (Maltz and Kohli, 1996; Moorman, 1995).

Furthermore, fit still remains one of the key concepts in organisation and management theory. Further development of different level of fit among various constructs will require researchers to devote more attention to their explorations and refinement. According to Weick (1995, p. 170), "Organizations were conceptualized as social structure that combine the generic subjectivity of interlocking routines, the inter-subjectivity of mutually reinforcing interpretations, and the movement back and forth between these two forms of communication". In the process of pursuing fit, the realisation of subjective-perceptual fit has proven to be at least as important as that of objective fit, especially when the concept of culture comes to play. Culture itself is sense making, which determines how the fit will be defined and perceived.

Finally, no research is perfect and complete in itself. Further efforts to improve and expand the existing study will always be needed. However, in view of this study purpose defined, this research seems to have fulfilled its objectives. The future will offer opportunities for further research of P-E fit and MO across cultures. This may provide theoretical and empirical grounds for these companies to function in a way that is more beneficial, not only by operating more effectively and thus contributing better to collectively, but also by having more satisfied organisational members with higher individual sense of well-being.

IV. Limitations

Most of the limitations of this study have been mentioned and discussed in several parts of this volume. They can be briefly classified as methodological, time and empirical limitations.

1. Methodological and time Limitations

First, the inherent limitations of research instruments, a self-report questionnaire administered in a cross-sectional fashion have been addressed by many researchers earlier. For example, Hansen and Kahnweiler (1997, p. 120) stated that the data collected through the positivistic use of questionnaire are "... static and do not capture contextual variance. Nor are self-reported measures able to penetrate unconscious or protective filters". Particularly, when the concept of culture is involved, one encounters great limitations because of unique features of a given culture cannot be studied by standardised questionnaires (Drenth and Groenendijk, 1984).

Second, the possibility of bias deriving from the tendency of responding to give "social-desirability" biased answers cannot be ruled out, especially for oriental and unsecured expatriate study sample (in the Gulf). The degrees of satisfaction and commitment might be inflated, and the P-E perceptions distorted. Hence, research results should be interpreted cautiously.

The common method bias may represent the third methodological limitation of this study. The P-E fit constructs (preference and perceived reality) as well as attitudinal outcomes (satisfaction and commitment) were all gathered from the same respondent. Therefore, the data may be affected by the common method bias. On the other hand, the common method bias is inevitable in this research design because it is the same individual's preference, perceived reality, satisfaction and commitment that were measured and analysed. bias can be overcome by using outcome performance measured by a third party or by other objective records. This brings up not only the feasibility limitation in the study's cultural context, but also the *time limitation*.

Finally, the study sample, Asians (mainly Indians) and Middle Eastern subjects were generally grouped together as eastern culture. Even thought it was made at the outset that it was the effects of 'national' cultures in addition to being expatriates that this might distort the results. Moreover, many nations are multicultural, and many cultures are multinational (Enz, 1988; Cooper and Denner, 1998; Sparrow, 2000). To overcome the complex nature of culture, a larger study sample of the employees may be used in a larger scale study.

2. Empirical Limitations

Since this study was conducted mainly within two multinational companies in Oman, it is not possible to generalise its results and conclusions to the whole population of relevant cultures. The results are probably valid only for the employees of the two companies only in Oman. However, it was not the objective of this study to make inferences based on research results regarding the entire population of the relevant cultures.

References

Adler, Nancy (1983a), "Cross-cultural Management Research: The Ostrich and the Trend," *Academy of Management Review*, 8, 3, pp. 226-232.

Adler, Nancy (1983b), "Typology of Management Studies involving Culture," *Journal of International Business Studies*, fall, pp. 29-47.

Adler, Nancy (1984), Understanding the Ways of Understanding: Cross-Cultural Management Methodology Reviewed," in Farmer, R. (ed.), *Advances in International Cooperative Management*, 1, 3, pp. 31-67.

Adler, Nancy (2002), *International Dimensions of Organizational Behavior*, 4th ed., Ohio, South-Western.

Adler, Nancy and Borys, Bryan (1996), "Two Types of Bureaucracy: Enabling and Coersive," *Administrative Science Quarterly*, 41, pp. 61-81.

Ajzen, I. and Fishbein, M. (1980), *Understanding Attitudes and Predicting Social Behavior*, Englewood Cliffs, NJ, Prentice-Hall.

Antonakis, John et al. (2003), "Context and Leadership: An Examination of the Nine-Factor Full-Range Leadership Theory Using the Multifactor Leadership Questionnaire," *Leadership Quarterly*, 14, pp. 261-295. ""

Antonakis, J. et al. (2004), "Methods for Studying Leadership," in Antonakis, J. et al. (eds.) *The Nature of Leadership*, Thousand Oaks, CA, Sage.

Barlett, Christopher A. and Goshal, S. (1989), *Managing Across Borders: The Transnational Solution*, Boston, MA, Harvard Business School.

Barlett, Christopher A. and Goshal, S. (2000), *Transnational Management: Text, Cases and Readings in Cross-Boarder Management*, 3rd ed., Boston, MA, McGraw Hill.

Barney, J.B. (1991), "Firm Resources and Sustained Competitive Advantage," *Journal of Management*, 17, 1, pp. 99-120.

Barrett, G.V. and Bass, B.M. (1976), "Cross-Cultural Issues in Industrial and Organizational Psychology," in Dunnette M.D. (ed.) *Handbook of Industrial and Organizational Psychology*, Chicago, Rand McNally College Publishing.

Bass, B. (1985), Leadership *and Performance beyond Expectations*, New York, Free Press.

Bass, B. and Avolio, B.J. (1994), *Improving Organizational Effectiveness through Transformational leadership*, Thousand Oaks, CA, Sage.

Berry, L.L. and Parasuraman, A. (1991), *Marketing Services: Competing Through Quality*, New York, The Free Press.

Bettencourt, L.A. and Brown, S.W. (2003), "Role Stressors and Customer-Oriented Boundary-Spanning Behaviours in Service Organizations," *Journal of the Academy of Marketing Science*, 31, 4, pp. 394-408.

Bettencourt, L.A. Brown, S.W. and MacKenzie, S.B. (2005), "Customer-Oriented Boundary-Spanning Behaviours: A Test of Social Exchange Model of Antecedents," *Journal of Retailing*, 81, 2, pp. 141-157.

Bettencourt, L.A., Gwinner, K.P. and Meuter, M.L. (2001), "A comparison of Attitude, Personality and Knowledge Predictors of Service-Oriented Organizational Citizenship Behaviors," *Journal of Applied Psychology*, 86, 1, pp. 29-41.

Bhagat, R.S. et al. (1990), "Cross-Cultural Issues in Organizational Psychology: Emergent Trends and Directions for Research in the 1990s," in Cooper, C.L. and Robertson, I.T. (eds.) *International Review of Industrial and Organizational Psychology*, Volume 5, Chichester, John Wiley and Sons.

Bharadwaj, S. et al. (1993), "Sustainable Competitive Advantage in the Service Industries: A Conceptual Model and Research Propositions," *Journal of Marketing*, 57, 4, pp. 83-99. Boyacigiller, N.A. and Adler N. (1991), "The Parochial Dinosaur: Organizational Science in a Global Context," *Academy of Management Review*, 16, 2, pp. 262-289.

Blyton, Paul (2001), "The General and the Particular in cross-National Comparative Research," *Applied Psychology: An International Review*, 50, 4, pp.590-595.

Blyton, Paul and Turnbull, Peter (1996), *Reassessing Human Resource Management*, London, Sage.

Boyacigiller, N.A. and Adler N. (1991), "The Parochial Dinosaur: Organizational Science in a Global Context," *Academy of Management Review*, 16, 2, pp. 262-289.

Bratton, John and Gold, Jeffrey (2003), *Human Resource Management,-Theory and Practice*, New York, Palgrave Macmillan.

Bright, David and Miller, Susan (2005), *Management and Personal Development: An MBA Study Guide*, Hull, The University of Hull School of Business.

Brislin, Richard W. (1970), "Back-Translation for Cross-Cultural Research," Journal of Cross Cultural Psychology, 1, 185-216.

Brislin, Richard W. (1976), "Comparative Research Methodology: Cross-Cultural Studies," Journal of International Psychology, 11, 215-229.

Brislin, Richard W. (2000), *Understanding Culture's Influence on Behavior*, 2nd ed., New York, Harcourt College Publishers.

Brown, Tom J. et al. (2002), "The Customer Orientation of Service Workers: Personality Trait Effects on Self- and Supervisor Performance Ratings," *Journal of Marketing Research*, 39, 1, pp. 110-119.

Buchanan, David and Huczynski, Andrzej (2004), *Organizational Behaviour: An Introductory Text*, 5th ed., Essex, Pearson Education.

Burnes, B. (2000), *Managing Change: A Strategic Approach to Organizational Dynamics*, 3rd ed., London, Financial Times/Prentice Hall.

Burns, T. and Stalker, G.M. (1961), The *Management of Innovation*, London, Financial Tavistock.

Certo, S.C. (2000), *Modern Management*, 8th ed., Upper Saddle River, NJ, Prentice Hall.

Chatterjee, S.R. (2007). "Human Resource Management in India: 'Where From' and 'Where To?'", *Research and Practice in Human Resource Management*, 15, 2, pp. 92-103.

Chomsky, N. (1965), *Aspects of the Theory of Syntax*, Cambridge MA, M.I.T. University Press.

Collis, D.J. and Montgomery, C.A. (1995), "Competing on Resources: Strategy in the 1990s," *Harvard Business Review*, 73, 4, pp. 118-128.

Cooper, C.R. and Denner, J. 1998), "Theories Linking Culture and Psychology: Universal and Community-Specific Processes," *Annual Review of Psychology*, 49, pp. 559-584.

Conner, Daryl R. (1995), *Managing at the Speed of Change*, New York, Villard.

Crouch, Sunny and Housden, Matthew (1996), *Marketing Research for Managers*, Oxford, Butterworth-Heinemann.

Day, G.S. (1994), "The Capabilities of Market-Driven Organizations," *Journal of Marketing*, 58, 3, pp. 37-52.

Day, G.S. and Nedungadi, P. (1994), "Managerial Representations of Competitive Advantage," *Journal of Marketing*, 58, pp. 31-44.

Day, G.S. (2003), "Creating a Superior Customer-Relating Capabilities," *Marketing Science Institute Working Paper Series*, Report No. 03-101.

Deshpandé, R. and Farley, E. Jr. (1998), "Measuring Market Orientation: Generalisation and Synthesis," *Journal of Market Focused Management*, 2, pp. 213-232.

Deshpandé, R. and Webster, F.E. (1989), "Organizational Culture and Marketing: Defining the Research Agenda," *Journal of Marketing*, 53, 1, pp. 3-15.

Deshpandé, R., Farley, E. Jr. and Webster, F.E. Jr. (1993), "Corporate Culture, Customer Orientation and Innovativeness in Japanese Firms: A Quadra Analysis," *Journal of Marketing*, 57, pp. 23-27.

Dessler, Gary (2001), *Management-Leading People and Organizations in the 21ˢᵗ Century*, New Jersey, Prentice Hall.

Dibb, B. et al. (1994), *Marketing: Concepts and Strategies*, London, Houghton Mifflin.

Dorfman, P.W. and Howell, J.P. (1988), "Dimensions of National Culture and Effective Leadership Patters: Hofstede Revisited," *Advances in International Comparative Management*, 3, pp. 127-150.

Doyle, P. (1998), *Marketing Management and Strategy*, 2ⁿᵈ ed., London, Prentice Hall International.

Doz, Yves L. and Prahalad, C.K. (1987), *The Multinational Mission*, New York, Free Press.

Doz, Yves L. et al. (2002), *From Global to Metanational: How Companies Win in the Knowledge Economy*, Boston, MA, Harvard Business School.

Drabble, Margaret (1980), *The Middle Ground*, London, Weidenfeld and Nicolson, quoted in Kelliny, W. (ed.) (1994), *Surveys in Linguistics and Language Teaching II: Culture Awareness, Language Competence and Literature*. European University Studies, Linguistics XXI, Vol. 79, p. 11, Frankfurt, Peter Lang.

Drenth, P.J.D. and Groenendijk, B. (1984), Work and Organizational Psychology, John Wiley and Sons.

Drucker, P.F. (1954), *The Practice of Management*, New York, Harper and Row.

Drucker, P.F. (1967), *A Theory of Management Effectiveness*, New York, McGraw-Hill.

Duffy, M. E. (1987), "Methodological Triangulation: a Vehicle for Merging Quantitative and Qualitative Methods," *Image*, 9, 3, pp.130-133.

Earley, P.C. (1993), "East Meets West Meets Midwest: Further Explorations of Collectivistic and Individualistic Work Groups," *Academy of Management Journal*, 36, 2, pp. 319-348.

Edwards, Jeffrey R. (1996), "An Examination of Competing Versions of the Person-Environment Fit Approach to Stress," *Academy of Management Journal*, 39, 2, pp. 292-339.

Edwards, Jeffrey R. and Copper, Cary L. (1990), "The Person-Environment Fit Approach to Stress: Recurring Problems and Some Suggested Solutions," *Journal of Organizational Behavior*, 11, 4, pp. 293-307.

Edwards, Jeffrey R. and Rothbard, Nancy P. (1999), "Work and Family Stress and Well-Being: An Examination of Person-Environment Fit in the Work and Family Domains," *Organizational Behavior and Human Decision Processes*, 77, 2, pp. 85-129.

Enz, C.A. (1988), "The Role of Value Congruity in International Power," *Administrative Science Quarterly*, 32, 2, pp. 284-304.

Fahy, J. et al. (2000), "The Development and Impact of Marketing Capabilities in Central Europe," *Journal of International Business Studies*, 31, 1, pp. 63-81.

Felton, Arthur P. (1959), "Making the Marketing Concept Working," *Harvard Business Review*, 37, July/August, p. 55-65.

Ferraro, Gary (1990), *The Cultural Dimension of International Business*, New Jersey, Prentice Hall.

Fijneman, Y.A. et al. (1996), "Individualism-Collectivism: An Empirical Study of a Conceptual Issue," *Journal of Cross-Cultural Psychology*, 27, 4, pp. 381-402.

Fishbein, M. and Ajzen, I. (1975), *Belief, Attitude, Intention and Behavior*, Reading, MA: Addison-Wesley.

Freathy, Angus (2006), Interview of Angus, Nestlé, Assistant Vice-President, Corporate HR-Training and Learning on 22nd August 2006, La Tour-de-Peilz, Vevey, Switzerland

Fry, Louis, W. and Smith, Deborah, A. (1987), "Congruence, Contingency, and Theory Building," *Academy of Management Review*, 12, 1, pp. 117-132.

Galal, Ola (2008), "Nakheel Signs Up to Hypermarket Deal", *Arabian Business.com*, 10 July 2008, <http://www.arabianbusiness.com/524174-nakheel-signs-up-to-hypermarket-deal>, accessed on 10 July 2008.

Gaulis, Irene (1996); "A Balanced Perspective of Qualitative and Quantitative Approaches to Research in Applied Linguistics" in Kelliny, W. (ed.), *Contemporary Education: Special Issue on Applied Linguistics and Research Inquiry*, 40, 1, pp. 209-234.

Godo Research and Marketing Consultancy (2008), Hyper markets tighten grip in the Gulf, <http://www.zawya.com/story.cfm/sidZAWYA20080311071740/SecMain/pagRetail>, accessed on 21st March 2008.

Grant, R.M. (1991), "The Resource-Based Theory of Competitive Advantage: Implications for Strategy Formulation," *California Management Review*, 33, spring, pp. 114-135.

Grant, R.M. (1995), *Contemporary Strategy Analysis*, 2nd ed., Cambridge, MA, Blackwell.

Gray and Hooley, (2002), "Corridors of Influence in the Dissemination of Customer-Oriented Strategy to Customer Contact Service Employees," *Journal of Marketing*, 64, 2, pp. 35-50.

Greenley, G.E. and Foxall, G.R. (1997), "Multiple Stakeholder Orientation in UK Companies and the Implications for Company Performance," *Journal of Management Studies*, 34, pp. 259-284.

Greenley, G.E. and Foxall, G.R. (1998), "External Moderation of Associations among Stakeholder Orientations and Company Performance," *International Journal of Research in Marketing*, 15, 1, pp. 51-69.

Harrison, G. et al. (2000), "Cultural Influence on Adaptation to Fluid Workgroups and Teams," *Journal of International Business Studies*, 31, 3, pp. 489-505.

Hartline, M.D. et al. (2000), "Organizational Culture and Marketing: Defining the Research Agenda," *Journal of Marketing*, 53, 1, pp. 3-15.

Hatch, E. and Farhady, H. (1982), Research Design and Statistics for Applied Linguistics, London, Newbury House Publishers.

Hansen, C.D. and Kahnweiler, M.W. (1997), "Executive Managers: Cultural Expectations through Stories about Work," *Journal of Applied Management Studies*, 6, 2, pp. 117-138.

Hill, Charles W.L. (2000), *International Business: Competing in the Global Market Place*, New York, Irwin/McGraw Hill.

Hill, Charles W.L. (2003), Global Business, New York, Irwin/McGraw Hill.

Hofstede, Geert (1980), *Culture's Consequences: International Differences in Work-Related Values*, Thousand Oaks, CA, Sage Publications.

Hofstede, Geert (1983), "National Cultures in Four Dimensions: A Research-Based Theory of Cultural Differences among Nations," *International Studies of Management and Organization*, Spring/ Summer, pp. 46-74.

Hofstede, Geert (1989), "Organizing for Cultural Diversity," *European Management Journal*, 7, 4, 390-397.

Hofstede, Geert (1990), "Motivation, Leadership and Organization: Do American Theories Apply Abroad?" in Pugh, D.S. (ed.), *Organization Theory: Selected Readings*, 3rd ed., Harmondsworth, Penguin.

Hofstede, Geert (1991), *Culture and Organization: Software of the Mind*, New York, McGraw-Hill.

Hofstede, Geert (1994), *Uncommon Sense about Organizations: Cases, Studies and Field Observations*, Thousand Oaks, CA, Sage Publications.

Hofstede, Geert (1996), *Cultures and Organizations: Software of the Mind: Intercultural Cooperation and its Importance for Survival*, New York, McGraw-Hill.

Homburg, C. and Pflesser, C. (2000), "A Multiple-Layer Model of Market-Oriented Organizational Culture: Measurement Issues and Performance Outcomes," *Journal of Marketing Research*, 37, 4, pp. 449-462.

Hooley et al. (1998), "Competitive Positioning and the Resource Based View of the Firm" *Journal of Strategic Marketing*, 6, 2, pp. 97-115.

Houston, Franklin S. (1986), "The Marketing Concept: What it is and what it is not," Journal of Marketing, 50, April, pp. 81-87.

Hunt, S.D. and Morgan, R.M. (1996), "The Resource-Advantage Theory of Competition: Dynamics, Path Dependencies and Evolutionary Dimensions," *Journal of Marketing*, 60, 4, pp. 107-114.

Jackson, M.C. (2003), Systems Thinking: Creative Holism for Managers, Chichester, Wiley.

Jaworski, B.J. and Kohli, A.K. (1993), "Market Orientation: Antecedents and Consequences," *Journal of Marketing*, 57, 3, pp. 53-70.

Jaworski, B.J. and Kohli, A.K. (1996), "Market Orientation: Review, Refinement and Roadmap," *Journal of Market Focused Management*, 1, pp. 119-35.

Jick, T. (1983), "Mixing Qualitative and Quantitative Methods: Triangulation in Action," in Van Maanen, J. (ed.) (1983). *Qualitative Methodology*, Beverly Hills, Sage.

Kamoche, K. (1996), "Strategic Human Resource Management within a Resource-Capability View of the Firm," *Journal of Management Studies*, 33, 2, pp. 213-233.

Kashani, Kamran (1996), "Marketing's Role is Changing to Survive?", *Journal of Long Range Planning*, 28, 4, pp. 263-274.

Keegan, Warren J. (1995), *Global Marketing Management*, New Jersey, Prentice Hall International.

Kelliny, W. (ed.) (1994), *Surveys in Linguistics and Language Teaching II: Culture Awareness, Language Competence and Literature*. European University Studies, Linguistics XXI, Vol. 79, Frankfurt, Peter Lang.

Kelliny, W. (ed.) (1996), *Contemporary Education: Special Issue on Applied Linguistics and Research Inquiry, 40, 1, pp. 131-146.*

Kennedy, K.N. et al. (2002), "Customer Mind-Set of Employees Throughout the Organization," *Journal of the Academy of Marketing Science*, 30, 2, pp. 159-171.

Kikrman, B.L. and Shapiro, D.L. (1997), "The Impact of Cultural Values on Employees Resistance to Teams: Toward a Model of Globalized Self-Managing Work Team Effectiveness," *Journal of Applied Management Studies*, 6, 2, pp. 117-138.

Kohli, A.K. and Jaworski, B.J. (1990), "Market Orientation: The Construct, Research Propositions and Managerial Implications," *Journal of Marketing*, 54, pp. 1-18.

Kotler, Philip and Keller, Kevin Lane (2006), *Marketing Management*, New Jersey, Pearson-Prentice Hall.

Kroeber, A.L. and Kulckhohn, C. (1952), "Culture: A Critical Review of its Concepts and Definitions," *Papers of Peabody Museum of American Archeology and Ethnology*, 47, 1, Cambridge, Harvard University Press.

Lasserre, Philippe (2003), *Global Strategic Management*, New York, Palgrave Macmillan.

Laurent, A. (1986), "The Cross-Cultural Puzzle of Global Human Resource Management," *Human Resource Management*, 25, 1, pp. 133-148.

Le Compte , M. and Goetz, J. (1982) "Problems of Reliability and Validity in Ethnographic Reseach," *Review of Educational Research*, 52, pp.31-60.

Lee, Yih-Teen (2003), "Display between Policy and Reality in Organizations in China: Toward a Theory of Strategic Hypocrisy," Paper presented at the 19th EGOS Colloquium, July, Copenhagen, Denmark.

Lee, Yih-Teen and Calvez, Vincent (2004), "Spontaneous Authenticity and the Analysis of Contemporary Aphorism in China: A Culturally-Adopted Quantitative Research Method," Paper presented at the International Conference: Crossing Frontiers in Quantitative and Qualitative Research Methods, AOM, Lyon, France.

Leonard-Barton, D. (1992), "Core Capabilities and Core Rigidities: A Paradox in Managing New Product Development," *Strategic Management Journal*, 13, pp. 111-125.

Lincoln, J.R. et al. (1981), "Cultural Orientations and Individual Reactions to Organizations: A Study of Employees in Japanese Owned Firms," *Administrative Science Quarterly*, 28, pp. 93-115.

Lincoln, J.R. et al. (1986), "Organizational Structure in Japanese and U.S. Manufacturing," *Administrative Science Quarterly*, 31, pp. 338-364.

Lincoln, J.R. and Kalleberg, A.L. (1990), *Culture, Control and Commitment: A Study of Work Organization and Attitudes in the United States and Japan*, Cambridge, Cambridge University Press.

Maltz, E. and Kohli, A.K. (1996), "Market Intelligence Dissemination Across Functional Boundaries," *Journal of Marketing Research*, 33, 1, pp. 47-61.

McMahon, Fred (2006), Director, "Oman's Growing Importance in World Souk," *Oman Daily Observer: Oman Money*, March, 61, p. 21, Oman, Muscat.

Meglino, B.M. and Ravlin, E.C. (1998), "Individual Values in Organizations: Concepts, Controversies, and Research," *Journal of Management*, 24, 3, pp. 351-389.

Miller, D. (1990), "Organisational Configurations: Cohesion, Change and Prediction," *Human Relations*, 43, pp. 771-789.

Ministry of National Economy (2004), "'Census 2003', Muscat Governorate Final results," *A Monthly Bulletin*, Muscat, The Administration of the 2003 Census of Population, Housing and Establishment, Fifth Edition, August 2004.

Ministry of Manpower (2008), *Database for Employment in the Private Sector in Oman*, accessed on 12 May 2008, Muscat, Oman.

Mintzberg, H. (1973), *The Nature of Managerial Work*, New York, Harper and Row.

Mintzberg, H. (1990), "The Manager's Job: Folklore and Fact," in Pugh, D.S. (ed.), Organization Theory: Selected Readings, 3rd ed., Harmondsworth, Penguin.

Moorman, C. (1995), "Organizational Market Information Processes: Cultural Antecents and New Product Outcomes," *Journal of Marketing Research*, 37, 2, pp. 318-335.

Moorman, R.H. and Blakely, G.L. (1995), "Individualism-Collectivism as an Individual Difference Predictor of Organizational Citizenship Behaviour," *Journal of Organizational Behaviour*, 16, 2, pp. 127-142.

Narver, J.C. and Slater, S. (1990), "The Effect of Market Orientation on Business Profitability," *Journal of Marketing*, 54, pp. 20-35.

Needham, Dave and Dransfield, Rob (1995), *Marketing-Everybody's Business*, Oxford, Heinemann.

Nestlé (2000), *People Building Brands*, Vevey, Switzerland, Nestlé S.A.

Olavarrieta, S. and Friedmann, R. (1999), "Market-Oriented Culture, Knowledge-Related Resources, Reputational Assets and Superior Performance: A Conceptual Framework," *Journal of Strategic Marketing*, 7, 4, pp. 215-228.

Oman Economic Review (2008), "Inflation Settles In", *Oman Economic Review*, 16 August 2008, <http://www.zawya.com/story.cfm?id=ZAWYA20080810064957&l=060143080815&zawyaemailmarketing> Accessed on 16 August, 2008

Oman Tribune (2008), *LuLu Plans RO70m in Investment for Five Projects*, 16 March 2008, p. 3.

Palmer, Adrian and Hartley, Bob (1996), *The Business and Marketing Environment*, Bath, McGraw Hill.

Porter, Michael E. (1980), *Competitive Strategy: Techniques for Analysing Industries and Competitors*, New York, Free Press.

Porter, Michael E. (1985), *Competitive Advantage: Creating and Sustaining Superior Performance*, New York, Free Press.

Porter, Michael E. (1986), *Competition in Global Industries*, Boston, MA, Harvard Business School Press.

Porter, Michael E. (1996), "What is Strategy?" *Harvard Business Review*, 74, November-December, pp. 61-78.

Prahalad, C.K. and Doz, Y.L. (1987), *The Multinational Mission: Balancing Local Demands and Global Vision*, New York, Free Press.

Prahalad, C.K. and Hamel, G. (1990), "The Core Competence of the Corporation," *Harvard Business Review*, 68, pp. 79-91.

Pugh, D.S., (ed.) (1990a), *Organization Theory: Selected Readings*, 3rd ed., Harmondsworth, Middlesex, Penguin Books.

Pugh, D.S. (1990b), "The Measurement of Organization Structure: Does Context Determine Form?" in Pugh, D.S. (ed.), *Organization Theory: Selected Readings*, 3rd ed., Harmondsworth, Penguin.

Punt, Trevor (2006), "Stereotypes: The Marketer," *Middle East: Mice & Events*, 3, October, p.55.

Ralston, D.A. et al. (1997), "The Impact of National Culture and Economic Ideology on Managerial Work Values: A Study of the United States, Russia, Japan and China," *Journal of International Business Studies*, 28, 1, pp. 177-207.

Robert, C. et al. (2000), "Empowerment and Continuous Improvement in the United States, Mexico, Poland and India: Predicting Fit on the Basis of the Dimensions of Power Distance and Individualism," *Journal of Applied Psychology*, 85, 5, pp. 643-658.

Roberts, K.H. (1970), "On Looking at an Elephant: An Evaluation of Cross-Cultural Research Related to Organizations," *Psychological Bulletin*, 74, 5, pp. 327-350.

Rokeach, R.W. (1973), *The Nature of Human Values*, New York, Free Press.

Rousseau, D.M. and Fried, Y. (2001), "Location, Location, Location: Contextualization of Organizational Research," *Journal of Organizational Behaviour*, 22, pp. 1-13.

Ruekert, R.W. (1992), "Developing a Market Orientation: An Organizational Strategy Perspective," International *Journal of Research in Marketing*, 9, 3, pp. 225-245.

Schneider, B. and White, S.S. (2004), *Service Quality: Research Prespectives*, Thousands Oak, CA: Sage Publications.

Schneider, B., White, S.S. and Paul, M.C. (1998), "Linking Service Climate and Customer Perceptions of Service Quality: Test of a Casual Model," *Journal of Applied Psychology, 83*, 2, pp. 150-163.

Schoemaker, P.J.H. (1992), "How to Link Strategic Vision to Core Capabilities," *Sloan Management Review*, 34, fall, pp. 67-81.

Senge, P.M. (1990), *The Fifth Discipline – The Art and Practice of the Learning Organization*, London, Random House.

Shenkar, O. and Von Glinow, M.A. (1994), "Paradoxes of Organizational Theory and Research: Using the Case of China to Illustrate National Contingency," *Management Science*, 40, 1, pp. 55-71.

Simon, Jon, Vosseberg, Gabriel and Levett, Brian (2001) Research Methods: An MBA Study Guide, Hull, the University of Hull Business School.

Slater, S. and Narver, J.C. (1994), "Does Competitive Environment Moderate the Market Orientation-Performance Relationship?" *Journal of Marketing*, 58, pp. 46-55.

Sparrow, L.M. (2000), "Beyond Multicultural Man: Complexities of Identity," International *Journal of Intercultural Relations*," 24, pp. 173-201.

Smith, P.B. et al. (1996), "National Culture and the Values of Organizational Employees," *Journal of Cross-Cultural Psychology*, 27, 2, pp. 231-264.

Stogdill, R.M. (1974), Handbook of Leadership: A Survey of the Literature, New York, Free Press.

Tayeb, M.H. (2001), "Conducting Research across Cultures: Overcoming Drawbacks and Obstacles," *International Journal of Cross-Cultural Management*, 1, 1, pp. 91-108.

Theweek (2008), Five more Projects from LuLu Group, Theweek, 264, 8, March 27, p.3.

Usunier, Jean-Claude (1996), *Marketing Across Cultures*, Europe, Prentice Hall.

Verdin, Paul and van Heck, Nick (2001), *From Local Champions to Global Masters: A Strategic Perspective on Managing Internationalism*, London, Palgrave Macmillan.

Venkatraman, N. and Camillus, John, C. (1984), "Exploring the Concept of 'Fit' in Strategic Management," *Academy of Management Review*, 9, pp. 513-525.

Weick, K.E. (1995), *Sensemaking in Organization*, London, Sage.

Woodward, J. (1965), *Industrial Organization: Theory and Practice*, Oxford, Oxford University Press.

Yip, George (1992), Total Global Strategy: Managing for Worldwide Competitive Advantage, Englewood Cliffs, Prentice-Hall.

Appendix A
CUSTOMER QUESTIONNAIR

Personal Data

Please, tick (√) where appropriate.

1) Nationality:

    i) Omani   (....)   ii) Non-Omani (....)

    iii) If non-Omani, please, specify:

    Arabic-speaker   (....)   **Indian**   (....)

    Asian   (....)   **Westerner**   (....)

    Other, please specify _____

2)   **Please state the town and area where you live in Oman:**

    i) Mattrah, Darsait, Ruwi   (....)

    ii) Al Quorum, Al Sarouj, Al Ealaam   (....)

    iii) North & South Ghubra, Ghala, Al Azaiba and Al Khuwair

                 (....)

    iv) Al Hail and Al Seeb   (....)

    v) North and South Al Mubeela, and Barka   (....)

Marketing Information

3) What are your criteria in choosing to shop in a hypermarket/supermarket?

Please, rank   (1= The most favourable, 2 = Favourable; 3 = Uncertain; 4 = Favourable;
5 = The least favourable).

No.	Customers' Perception	1	2	3	4	5
i	Low prices					
ii	Variety of brands and prices					
iii	Quality of Service					
iv	Availability of special products & delicatessen					
v	Convenient location					
vi	Monthly discounts and special offers					

Please, rank   (1= The most favourable, 2 = Favourable; 3 = Uncertain; 4 = Favourable;
5 = The least favourable).

No.	Customers' Perception	1	2	3	4	5
vii	Seasonal discounts (e.g. return to school and Month of Ramadan)					
viii	Discounted prices on certain products (e.g. Carrefour's Vendors', LuLu's clothes and electronics)					
ix	Wholesale and family size products					
x	Raffles and prizes (e.g. cars)					
xii	Earning points and rewards card					

4) Please choose the hypermarket(s)/supermarket(s) where you find:

No.	Quality	Carrefour 1	LuLu 2	Carrefour & Lulu 3	Others 4
i	Best value for money				
ii	Best service				
iii	Best products				
iv	Special products				
v	Best raffles and prizes				

5) Please identify your favourite hypermarket/supermarket:

         i) Carrefour   (....)
         ii) LuLu   (....)
         iii) Other hypermarket/supermarket   (....)

6) Please identify the frequency of the use, the availability and the quality of the facility by Your Favourite Hypermarket/ Supermarket, you mentioned above.

No.	Quality	Always 1	Often 2	Sometimes 3	Never 4
i	Using Services				
ii	Availability of services				
iii	Getting the expected service				
iv	Having your complaints taken seriously				
v	Receiving satisfactory solutions or help				

7) **Do you have any other information or suggestions you want to add? Please, indicate below.**

_____

_____

_____

_____

_____

_____

8) **Any suggestions? Please, indicate below.**

_____

_____

_____

_____

_____

_____

Thank you for giving us some of your time and your kind participation.

Wafik Kelliny

Appendix B

STAFF QUESTIONNAIRE: BUSINESS CULTURAL VALUES

Thank you for participating in this research project. You will find below a series of descriptions concerning you and your company. Please, mark the extent to which you agree or disagree with these statements.

Please use *the past six months* as your point of reference, when rating statements concerning your company. Please, note that there is NO right or wrong answers. Just describe what you think and you feel as it is. We guarantee that your answers and personal data will be kept confidential.

Thank you for giving us some of your time and your kind participation.

Wafik Kelliny

In the following sections, we would like to know your preference, your perception of the actual situation, and your satisfaction about the way work is organised in your company. The same items will come up in all three sections. Please, mark your opinions by ticking ($\sqrt{}$) these items according to the focus of sections respectively.

Actual Situation in Your Company
Based on what I see in my company, I think that …

No.	Statement	Strongly Disagree 5	Disagree 4	Neutral 3	Agree 2	Strongly Agree 1
1	There are well-defined job descriptions for most people working in the company.					
2	Clear rules exist for reporting a problem occurring in the fulfilment of one's every day tasks.					
3	Written reports are often required for every day work.					
4	Employees of the company communicate through formally-designed channels.					
5	Employees have say in decisions concerning their work.					
6	Employees are free to communicate work-related information both upward and downward.					
7	Data and information necessary for fulfilling ordinary work are easily obtainable without going to supervisors.					
8	When someone notices superiors making a mistake, he/she is expected to give them feedback and criticism directly.					

Level of Your Satisfaction with the Actual Situation in Your Company

I am satisfied with the extent to which ....

No.	Statement	Strongly Disagree 5	Disagree 4	Neutral 3	Agree 2	Strongly Agree 1
9	There are well-defined job descriptions for most people working in the company.					
10	Clear rules exist for reporting a problem occurring in the fulfilment of one's every day tasks in the company.					
11	Written reports are often required for every day work in the company.					
12	Employees of the company communicate through formally-designed channels in the company.					
13	Employees have Say in decisions concerning their work in the company.					
14	Employees are free to communicate work-related information both upward and downward.					
15	Data and information necessary for fulfilling ordinary work are easily obtainable without going to supervisors in the company.					
16	When someone notices superiors making a mistake, he/she is expected to give them feedback and criticism in the company.					

How do you feel about your company?

Please, mark the extent to which you think the following statements characterise how you feel about your company.

No.	Statement	Strongly Disagree 1	Disagree 2	Neutral 3	Agree 4	Strongly Agree 5
17	I present this company as a great place to work in.					
18.	I am proud to tell others that I am part of this company.					
19.	This company really inspires me to perform my job to the best of my ability.					
20.	I really care about the interest of this company.					

Personal Data

21) I am:

i)	Omani	(....)
ii)	An Arabic-speaker/Middle Eastern	(....)
iii)	Indian	(....)
iv)	Asian	(....)
v)	African	(....)
vi)	A westerner	(....)
	Other, please specify	

_____

22) Education:

What is your highest educational qualification/training?
    i) Vocational Training, Secondary School Certificate (Tawjihia)/
      Technical Diploma   (....)
    ii) Higher Technical Diploma (following secondary school) (....)
    iii) University Degree: B.A. or B.Sc.   (....)
    iv) Master's Degree   (....)
    v) Ph.D.   (....)

23) Job Level:

What is your job level in the company?
    i)   Non-management   (....)
    ii) Lower management   (....)
    iii) Middle management   (....)
    iv) Top management   (....)

24) I work for:

i)   Carrefour   (....)
ii) LuLu   (....)

**4) Do you have any other information or suggestions you want to
   add? Please, indicate below.**

_____

_____

_____

_____

_____

_____

5) Any suggestions? Please, indicate below.

_____

_____

_____

_____

_____

_____

Thank you for giving us some of your time and your kind participation.

Wafik Kelliny

Appendix C

Semi-Structured Interviews for Global Retailers and Suppliers

---

The writer assured the interviewee that:

- The collected data will be used collectively for research purposes only
- This research is solely associated with UK studies and research, not Oman or the Gulf
- Confidentiality of responses, personal data or views will be kept and these will be used collectively for research purposes only.
- There is no right or wrong answer

In so doing, the interviewees were also assured that this research was not associated in any way with the Ministry of Manpower of the Sultanate of Oman or any other Omani governmental body, if the need arises. This was to avoid any bias.

1) How does the top management conceive the role of marketing?

2) Please, describe the marketing function in terms of staff, centralised, decentralised responsibilities, etc.?

3) What are the relationships of marketing with other functions such as acquiring brands and non-brands, local products, R&D, finance in your branch/company?

4) What are the contributions of the functions such as processing data; finance; R&D; acquisition of different products, brands and makes; as well as production in establishing marketing principles in your branch/ company?

5) How do you find relationships between marketers, clients, suppliers and competitors?

6) Who are your company's main competitors in Oman? What are your company's strengths and weaknesses compared to them?

7) Does your company have a long term plan which is fitting within the corporation's long term strategies? If yes, what shape does this marketing plan take and what are the objectives in terms of domestic and international marketing?

8) What is the process of decision making within the company in the domain of marketing?

9) How do you decide market segmentation, distribution channels, pricing, advertising, cost problems and evaluation of marketing strategies when implemented?

10) What kind of market research does your company conduct? Is it the most important element in making decisions?

11) Do you have other sources of information beside market research? How much of it is produced by the sales force; by consultants; by professional organizations and by other sources?

12) How much is made of marketing publications, marketing consultants compared to your own ideas and intuitions?

13) How and where do new ideas emerge in your company regarding new products, new markets, revitalisation of old products (by R&D, top management, customers, etc.)?

14) Could you underline marketing approaches which are typical of your company/branch, which differ from the practices of some of your direct competitors?

15) Who is involved in the formulation and decision-making regarding strategies of different elements produced or sold within your company (suppliers, brands, etc.)?

16) Which are the most important consumer segments for your products in Oman?

17) Do you see Oman as a single market or a set of heterogeneous markets?

18) Could you explain the structure of you distribution system in this branch or other areas of Muscat, other areas of Oman, Gulf countries, the Middle East or other parts of the world?

19) What is the role of the Logistics Department?

20) What is the role of the IT Department in terms of identifying customers' buying patterns, etc.?

21) What is the process of decision making regarding pricing of your company's products in Oman and abroad?

22) On which basis are the prices for each market (or retailer) decided and who decides them?

23) Could you (as a retailer or supplier) explain the structure of your distribution system in Oman and abroad?

24) By whom and how is your supplier system managed in Oman and abroad?

25) How were the ideas of your most successful product emerged (through R&D, top management, clients, etc.)?

26) In your view, is the process of launching a new product the same in Oman as in other countries in the Gulf, the Middle East or other parts of the world? What differences do you see if any?

27) What methods do you use to measure consumer satisfaction?

28) How do you deal with consumer complaints?

29) How do you evaluate the efficiency of your company's/branch' marketing policies?

30) How has marketing evolved within your company/branch during the last ten years?

31) What is the role of the top management and the firm's leadership in terms of supporting the marketing strategies and the business network in Oman and abroad?

32) Additional information.

33) Any Suggestions?

Thank you for giving us some of your time and your kind participation.

Wafik Kelliny

Appendix D (Part 1)
Asset-Based, Competitiveness and Extended Marketing Mix (P1-8)
of Global Hypermarkets and Supermarkets in Oman

Global Retailer	Carrefour Hypermarkets and Shopping Centres (Global French-Franchised Owned by Emirati Group)	Lulu Hypermarkets and Supermarkets (Global South Indian Group)	Al Safeer Hyper-market & Supermarkets (Gulf Company Owned by Emirati Group)	The Sultan Centre & Super-market (Al Jumlah) (Gulf Company Owned by a Kuwaiti Group)	Al Fair Supermarkets (Global Spinneys' Franchised Group, Owned by Emirati Group)
Positioning and Background Information	• *Market leader* • Middle market sector (but low price of a basket of goods) • Carrefour's and other international brands • Segment: Omani large and extended families • Niche: Middle class: expatriates, European, Arab and Asian elites • Marketing strategy: Minimum profit, often some losses with fruits and vegetables, fast turn over of products, not sold electronics returned to suppliers after 60 days. • Largest shopping centre, becoming an outing for Omani and non-Omani families. • Service standard and HRs' attitude is an *asset which other retailers have not been successful or interested in imitating.*	• First competitor • Discount market sector • Lulu's lower level brand, other Asian and international brands of a variety of prices • Segment: Omani large and extended families and South Indians • Niche: North Indians and other expatriates, for convenience and lower prices • Marketing strategy: Second big and fast turn over of a variety of low cost products, but poor presentation of cheap fruits and vegetables.	• Second competitor • Middle market sector, low cost and lower quality of Asian and international brands of a variety of prices • Segment: Omani large and extended families in the neighbourhood and North Indians • Niche: Other expatriates in the neighbourhoods • Marketing strategy: Steady turn over of products.	• Third competitor • *Premium market* sector • Quality delicatesse and international brands as well as Sultan's few brands • Segment: Middle and upper middle classes of Omanis and Expatriates • Niche: Other middle class expatriates (Loyal and convenience shoppers) • Marketing strategy: Steady turn over of products. • **N.B.** Opened lately second *but discount branch* near Carrefour's first branch targeting lower income extended Omani families and expatriates from Muscat and other regions of Oman. It is called "Al Jumlah", which means 'wholesale'. High turn over of products, but poor presentation.	• Struggling competitor (Reminding of K-Mart's case) • Premium market sector • Spinneys and other international brands • Segment: Upper middle classes of expatriates buying small quantities, focusing on Dutch, British and Americans in the respective neighbourhoods/branches • Niche: Upper middle classes of Omanis in the neighbourhoods • Marketing strategy: Slow turn over of products and partly empty shelves.

Appendix D (Part 2)
Asset-Based, Competitiveness and Extended Marketing Mix (P1-8) of
Global Hypermarkets and Supermarkets in Oman

Global Retailer	Carrefour Hypermarkets and Shopping Centres	Lulu Hypermarket and Supermarkets	Al Safeer Hypermarket & Supermarkets	The Sultan Center & Supermarket (Al Jumlah)	Al Fair Supermarkets (Franchised Spinneys)
Product (P1)	• Wide range of middle and high quality of Carrefour products and international brands, as well as Omani products/packed products. • Carrefour brands and products. • During expansion ends, and holiday seasons targeting low-income Asian window-shoppers with low quality and cheap products	• Wide range of products and brands produced in India, China and the west as well as products/packed products in Oman. • Lulu's brands produced in India, China and Asia. • Poorly presented low price fruit and vegetables.	• Wide range of products and brands produced in India, China and the west as well as products/packed products in Oman.	• Middle and high quality products and brands, as well as Omani products/packed products. • Quality brands for high income clients. • Special and authentic Middle Eastern and European products and delicatesse for Omani elites and high income Arab expats.	• Limited range of middle and high quality products and brands, as well as Omani products/packed products. • Accepting individual orders from high income and specific/individual needs: Importing fresh orders for Christmas, e.g. Christmas trees, turkeys and pork, as well as special products/orders for Dutch expatriates.
Pricing (P2)	• Lower price of a basket of medium and quality products. • Using information processing data: prices may vary during the day, weekdays, beginning or end of the month according to customer's behaviour or buying power/pattern.	• Wide range of prices; low prices are available according to quality and country of production. • Prices of some products are lowered during promotion periods.	• Wide range of prices; low prices are available according to quality • Prices of a few products are lowered during promotion periods.	• Middle and high range of prices, according to quality and brands. • Prices of a few products are lowered during promotion periods.	• Superficial lowering of prices, during the weekly 'Monday Market Day' and post-Christmas promotion period. • Sometimes, prices are lowered following the Christmas season, but not entered into the system resulting in customers paying the original price, if the customer is not alert due to buying a small amount.

Appendix D (Part 3)
Asset-Based, Competitiveness and Extended Marketing Mix (P1-8) of
Global Hypermarkets and Supermarkets in Oman

Global Retailer	Carrefour Hypermarkets and Shopping Centres	Lulu Hyper-market and Super-markets	Al Safeer Hyper-market & Super-markets	The Sultan Center & Super-market (Al Jumlah)	Al Fair Super markets (Franchised Spinneys)
Promotion (P3)	• The retail *business has been described as seasonal* in Oman, e.g. the first ten days of the month, the Islamic month of Ramadan, Eids or Islamic feasts, end of May and June before expatriates holiday and 'Back to School' season. • Promotion leaflets are delivered to the homes advertising for good shopping opportunities. • This was not applicable to the month of Ramadan in 2006, when prices went up. • Raffles are on *a small scale* to encourage spending more.	• The retail business has been described as *seasonal* in Oman. • Promotions and leaflets are delivered to the homes imitating Carrefour's promotion strategy. • This was not applicable to the month of Ramadan in 2006, when prices went up. . • Raffles on *a large scale* are also used to encourage spending more: Offering large number of cars as well as all sorts of electronic equipment.	• The rtail business has been described as *seasonal* in Oman. • Promotions and leaflets are delivered to the homes imitating Carrefour's promotion strategy. • Raffles are on *a smaller scale* than in Lulu Hypermarket and supermaerkets to encourage spending more.	The retail business has been described as *seasonal* in Oman. Promotions and leaflets are delivered to the homes imitating Carrefour's promotion strategy. Raffles are on *a smaller scale*, but cannot be compared to Lulu's or Safeer's.	• Taking into account the low business, promotions, discounts or raffles are unaffordable or artificial. • Superficial lowering of prices, during the weekly 'Monday Market Day' and post-Christmas promotion season. • No raffles, due to different types of customers and being unable to afford them.

Appendix D (Part 4)
Asset-Based, Competitiveness and Extended Marketing Mix (P1-8)
of Global Hypermarkets and Supermarkets in Oman

Global Retailer	Carrefour Hypermarkets and Shopping Centres	Lulu Hypermarket and Supermarkets	Al Safeer Hyper-market & Super-markets	The Sultan Center & Supermarket (Al Jumlah)	Al Fair Supermarkets (Franchised Spinneys)
Place (P4)	• First branch is located in the outskirt of Muscat with a large parking space. Carrefour is presently expanding by building a multistory car park and additional shopping premises, to overcome being the 'victim of its own success'. • More hypermarkets to be opened in the center of Muscat, near the Sultan Center and in Sohar which is in Al Batinah Region with the highest density of population. • Lulu has recently opened a supermarket in Sohar. There is now a sizable community of Asian and western expatriates, due to its new port and aluminium factory.	• First super-market in Salalah, then it was granted permission, with difficulty, to open a hypermarket in the heart of Muscat, followed by a supermarket in Darsit where the highest density of Indians & Asians resides. • Opened a supermarket in Sohar in Al Batinah Region with the highest density of Omani population. There is now a sizable community of Asian and western expatriates, due to Sohar' new port and aluminum factory.	• Al Safeer Hypermarke t and supermarket s are found where high density of Omani population resides either in Muscat or other regions such as Barka and Nizwa. This does not exclude targeting nearby Asian, Arabic speaking and western expatriates.	• The Sultan Center is located in the heart of Muscat near the residence and work places of expatriate and Omani high income groups. • Al Jumlah supermarket was opened next to Carrefour at the outskirt of Muscat near low income population and weekly shoppers from other regions. • Carrefour is about to open a new hypermarket near the Sultan Center.	• Supermarkets of different sizes are scattered in many areas of Muscat. • Al Fair supermarket in Salalah closed down a few months after the opening of Lulu supermarket in Salalah. • One more Al fair supermarket closed down in Muscat, but two others opened in other parts of Muscat area.

Appendix D (Part 5)
Asset-Based, Competitiveness and Extended Marketing Mix (P1-8)
of Global Hypermarkets and Supermarkets in Oman

Global Retailer	Carrefour Hypermarkets and Shopping Centres	Lulu Hypermarket and Supermarkets	Al Safeer Hyper-market & Supermarkets	The Sultan Center & Super-market (Al Jumlah)	Al Fair Super-markets (Franchised Spinneys)
People and Marketing Mix (P5)	• Top management is discretely around (The present general manager is British of Sudanese origin), and the assistant manager is Indian with long experience with Spinneys in Bahrain. • Heads of sections are available for customer service and staff support • Staffs including section heads represent a mix of Arabic speakers and Indians, most of them are experienced, friendly, and helpful giving a professional impression. (Arabic speaking staff receives higher salaries and benefits than Asian colleagues.) • Omanisation is taking place. Omani staff are gradually learning and trying to adapt to Carrefour's organisational culture. • *Carrefour is the only retailer making maximum use of peoples' potential, as an asset–based, or a vital element of the marketing mix.*	• Top management and most heads of sections are Indians with experience in India or the Gulf. • Groups of staff are seen walking to work, which is not the norm in the heat of Oman; other retailers transport their staff by mini-buses. This may result in a negative impression on part of the customers and having exhausted sweating staff reporting to work. • Heads of sections are available for customer service and staff support, but not at the same level as Carrefour • Most of the staff are South Indians and a handful of Philippines weighing vegetables and fruits next to a few Omani females. • Omanisation is taking place. Omani staff, mostly cashiers, are gradually learning and reluctantly adapting to Lulu's less demanding organisational culture.	• Top management and most heads of sections are Indians with experience in India or the Gulf. • Most of the staff are Indians, in addition to the same quota of Omani staff that need training and experience, as is the case in Lulu.	• Top management and most heads of sections are Arabic speakers with experience mainly in Kuwait or the Gulf. • Most of the staff are Arabic speakers and Indians, in addition to the same quota of Omani staff that need training and experience, as is the case in Lulu.	• Top management and most heads of sections are Indians with experience in India or the Gulf or both. • Most of the staff are Indians, in addition to the same quota of Omani staff that need training and experience, as is the case in Lulu. • Staff working, including Omanis, in Madinat Qaboos and CCC branches is the highest caliber with special training and most of all positive if not submissive attitudes towards customers. •

Appendix D (Part 6)
Asset-Based, Competitiveness and Extended Marketing Mix (P1-8) of Global Hypermarkets and Supermarkets in Oman

Global Retailer	Carrefour Hypermarkets and Shopping Centres	Lulu Hyper-market & Super-markets	Al Safeer Hyper-market	The Sultan Center & Supermarket (Al Jumlah)	Al Fair Supermarkets (Franchised Spinneys)
Process (P6)	• Expatriate staff and heads of sections are always available for customer service and react in a professional, friendly and efficient manner, meeting expectations. • The percentage of the Omani staff is nearly the same in the retail industry, but having a better attitude in Carrefour. • Carrefour can be described as a victim of its success, but it is expanding its tangible resources and overcoming difficulties through its dedicated heads of sections and staff, e.g. the manner and the speed of service.	•Expatriate staff and heads of sections are sometimes available for customer service, polite when directly approached. •Customers have lower expectations in terms of service compared to Carrefour's.	•Expatriate staff and heads of sections are also sometimes available for customer service, polite when directly approached. •Customers have lower expectations in terms of service, compared to Carrefour's.	•Expatriate staff and heads of sections are also sometimes available for customer service, polite when directly approached, but slightly better than in Lulu and Al Safeer.	• In Madinat Qaboos and CCC branches, the customers who are mostly the expatriate and Omani elites receive personal and sometimes royal level of service. • *On the other hand, in the other branches* minimum staff is available providing minimum level of service to customers who are buying a few items, probably for convenience reasons.
Personal Services and Quality (P7)	• Customer service is an asset which is well exploited, even when Carrefour is becoming the victim of its own success. Staff provides professional, friendly and efficient quality service. • Carrefour makes maximum use of this intangible asset, which is difficult to imitate.	•Minimum service, but polite. Meets customer's low expectations. •Focuses on car and electronic raffles.	•Minimum, but polite. Meets customer's expectations. •Focuses on car and electronic raffles.	•Average, but focuses on quality authentic products and delicatesse for high-income clients.	•Top quality and personalized type of service is limited to Madinat Qaboos and CCC branches, while minimum in other branches. •Quality of service in other branches has deteriorated over the last five years.
Processing Information (P8)	• Provides feedback of customers' behaviour and inventory during the day, week, months and seasons, *with immediate application* in terms of prices, services, inventory, etc.	•Seems to be used to identify seasonable periods.	•Maybe, but seasonable.	•Maybe seasonable.	• Inefficiently used. Many nearly-expired items regularly sold at reduced prices. In addition, partly empty shelves are found in most branches.
	Financial systems, including accountancy and inventory, are unified and standardised within each of the above-mentioned organisations or retailers, regardless of the geographical or international location.				

APPENDIX E

TABLES 4.1- 4.31

Table 4.1: Customers' Perception of the Importance of Low Prices

Scale* / Nationality	1	2	3	4	5	Total	Mode	Mean	Median	SD
Omani N	380	33	9	7	2	431	1	1.19	1	0.59
%	88.17	7.66	2.09	1.62	0.46	100				
Non-Omani N	347	28	22	4	6	407	1	1.27	1	0.74
%	85.26	6.88	5.41	0.98	1.47	100				
Total N	727	61	31	11	8	838	1	1.22	1	0.66
%	86.75	7.28	3.70	1.31	0.95	100				

*1= The most favourable, 2 = Favourable; 3 = Uncertain; 4 = Favourable; 5 = The least favourable).

Most Favourable: 1	Least Favourable: 5	d.f.: 4	Chi-Square (x²) 9.50	p=0.05

Table 4.2: Customers' Perception of the Importance of Brands and Prices Variety

Scale* / Nationality	1	2	3	4	5	Total	Mode	Mean	Median	SD
Omani N	387	27	7	4	6	431	1	1.18	1	0.63
%	89.79	6.26	1.62	0.93	1.39	100				
Non-Omani N	342	42	9	9	5	407	1	1.26	1	0.72
%	84.03	10.32	2.21	2.21	1.23	100				
Total N	729	69	16	13	11	838	1	1.22	1	0.68
%	86.99	8.23	1.91	1.55	1.31	100				

*1= The most favourable, 2 = Favourable; 3 = Uncertain; 4 = Favourable; 5 = The least favourable).

Most Favourable: 1	Least Favourable: 5	d.f.: 4	Chi-Square (x²) 7.62	p<0.25 (0.106)

Table 4.3: Customers' Perception of the Importance of Monthly Discounts and Special Offers

Scale* / Nationality	1	2	3	4	5	Total	Mode	Mean	Median	SD
Omani N	399	20	5	4	3	431	1	1.13	1	0.52
%	92.58	4.64	1.16	0.93	0.7	100				
Non-Omani N	64	297	10	13	23	407	2	2.10	2	0.90
%	15.72	72.97	2.46	3.19	5.65	100				
Total N	463	317	15	17	26	838	1	1.60	1	0.88
%	55.25	37.83	1.79	2.03	3.1	100				

*1 = The most favourable, 2 = Favourable; 3 = Uncertain; 4 = Favourable; 5 = The least favourable).

Most Favourable: 1	Least Favourable: 5	d.f.: 4	Chi-Square (x^2) 505.98	$p < 0.01$

Table 4.4: Customers' Perception of the Importance Seasonal Discounts (e.g., Return to School, Month of Ramadan)

Scale* / Nationality	1	2	3	4	5	Total	Mode	Mean	Median	SD
Omani N	340	70	11	6	4	431	1	1.29	1	0.67
%	78.89	16.24	2.55	1.39	0.93	100				
Non-Omani N	9	199	187	7	5	407	2	2.51	2	0.64
%	2.21	48.89	45.95	1.72	1.23	100				
Total N	349	269	198	13	9	838	1	1.88	2	0.89
%	41.65	32.1	23.63	1.55	1.07	100				

*1 = The most favourable, 2 = Favourable; 3 = Uncertain; 4 = Favourable; 5 = The least favourable).

Most Favourable: 1	Least Favourable: 5	d.f.: 4d.f.: 4	Chi-Square (x^2) 532.17	$p < 0.01$

Table 4.5: Customers' Perception of the Importance Discounted Prices on o (e.g., Carrefour's Vendors', LuLu's Clothes and Electronics)

Scale* Nationality	1	2	3	4	5	Total	Mode	Mean	Median	SD
Omani N	103	94	199	27	8	431	3	2.40	3.00	0.98
%	23.9	21.81	46.17	6.26	1.86	100				
Non-Omani N	22	40	233	107	5	407	3	3.08	3.00	0.79
%	5.41	9.83	57.25	26.29	1.23	100				
Total N	125	134	432	134	13	838	3	2.73	3.00	0.95
%	14.92	15.99	51.55	15.99	1.55	100				

*1= The most favourable, 2 = Favourable; 3 = Uncertain; 4 = Favourable; 5= The least favourable).

Most Favourable: 1	Least Favourable: 5	d.f.: 4	Chi-Square (x^2) 124.79	$p<0.01$

Table 4.6: Customers' Perception of the Importance of Wholesale and Family Size Products

Scale* Nationality	1	2	3	4	5	Total	Mode	Mean	Median	SD
Omani N	397	24	4	4	2	431	1	1.12	1	0.49
%	92.11	5.57	0.93	0.93	0.46	100				
Non-Omani N	70	60	111	100	66	407	3	3.08	3	1.31
%	17.2	14.74	27.27	24.57	16.22	100				
Total N	467	84	115	104	68	838	1	2.07	1	1.39
%	55.73	10.02	13.72	12.41	8.11	100				

*1= The most favourable, 2 = Favourable; 3 = Uncertain; 4 = Favourable; 5= The least favourable).

Most Favourable: 1	Least Favourable: 5	d.f.: 4	Chi-Square (x^2) 492.52	$p<0.01$

Table 4.7: Customers' Perception of the Importance of Raffles and Prizes

Scale* Nationality	1	2	3	4	5	Total	Mode	Mean	Median	SD
OmaniN	380	32	10	5	4	431	1	1.19	1	0.62
%	88.17	7.42	2.32	1.16	0.93	100				
Non-Omani N	270	110	16	4	7	407	1	1.45	1	0.77
%	66.34	27.03	3.93	0.98	1.72	100				
Total N	650	142	26	9	11	838	1	1.32	1	0.71
%	77.57	16.95	3.1	1.07	1.31	100				

*1=The most favourable, 2=Favourable; 3=Uncertain; 4=Favourable; 5=The least favourable).

Most Favourable: 1	Least Favourable: 5	d.f.: 4	Chi-Square (x^2) 63.14	$p<0.01$

Table 4.8: Customers' Perception of the Importance of Earning Points and Rewards Card

Scale* Nationality	1	2	3	4	5	Total	Mode	Mean	Median	SD
OmaniN	10	12	9	60	340	431	5	4.64	5	0.85
%	2.32	2.78	2.09	13.92	78.89	100				
Non-Omani N	15	13	116	98	165	407	5	3.95	4	1.07
%	3.69	3.19	28.5	24.08	40.54	100				
Total N	25	25	125	158	505	838	5	4.30	5	1.02
%	2.98	2.98	14.92	18.85	60.26	100				

*1=The most favourable, 2=Favourable; 3=Uncertain; 4=Favourable; 5=The least favourable).

Most Favourable: 1	Least Favourable: 5	d.f.: 4	Chi-Square (x^2) 161.86	$p<0.01$

Table 4.9: Customers' Perception of the Importance of Special Products

Scale* Nationality	1	2	3	4	5	Total	Mode	Mean	Median	SD
Omani N	90	94	70	55	122	431	2	3.06	3	1.52
%	20.88	21.81	16.24	12.76	28.31	100				
Non-Omani N	322	44	22	13	6	407	1	1.37	1	0.84
%	79.12	10.81	5.41	3.19	1.47	100				
Total N	412	138	92	68	128	838	1	2.24	2	1.50
%	49.16	16.47	10.98	8.11	15.27	100				

*1= The most favourable, 2 = Favourable; 3 = Uncertain; 4 = Favourable; 5 = The least favourable).

Most Favourable: 1	Least Favourable: 5		d.f.: 4	Chi-Square (x^2) 304.43	$p < 0.01$

Table 4.10: Customers' Perception of the Importance of Convenient Location

Scale* Nationality	1	2	3	4	5	Total	Mode	Mean	Median	SD
Omani N	42	73	111	107	98	431	2	3.34	3	1.27
%	9.74	16.94	25.75	24.83	22.74	100				
Non-Omani N	55	120	40	60	132	407	5	3.23	3	1.49
%	13.51	29.48	9.83	14.74	32.43	100				
Total N	97	193	151	167	230	838	5	3.29	3	1.38
%	11.58	23.03	18.02	19.93	27.45	100				

*1= The most favourable, 2 = Favourable; 3 = Uncertain; 4 = Favourable; 5 = The least favourable).

Most Favourable: 1	Least Favourable: 5	d.f.: 4	Chi-Square (x^2) 64.20	$p < 0.01$

Table 4.11: Customers' Perception of the Importance of Quality of Service

Scale* / Nationality	1	2	3	4	5	Total	Mode	Mean	Median	SD
Omani N	293	113	7	9	9	431	1	1.44	1	0.81
%	67.98	26.22	1.62	2.09	2.09	100				
Non-Omani N	317	72	7	7	4	407	1	1.30	1	0.68
%	77.89	17.69	1.72	1.72	0.98	100				
Total N	610	185	14	16	13	838	1	1.37	1	0.75
%	72.79	22.08	1.67	1.91	1.55	100				

*1 = The most favourable, 2 = Favourable; 3 = Uncertain; 4 = Favourable; 5 = The least favourable).

Most Favourable: 1	Least Favourable: 5	d.f.: 4	Chi-Square (x^2) 11.53	$p<0.05$

Table 4.12: Customers' Perception of Hypermarket Offering the Best Value for Money

Scale* / Nationality	1	2	3	4	5	Total	Mode	Mean	Median	SD
Omani N	93	281	49	8		431	2	1.94	2	0.63
%	21.58	65.20	11.37	1.86		100				
Non-Omani N	76	293	34	4		407	2	1.92	2	0.55
%	18.67	71.99	8.35	0.98		100				
Total N	169	574	83	12		838	2	1.93	2	0.59
%	20.17	68.5	9.9	1.43		100				

*1 = The most favourable, 2 = Favourable; 3 = Uncertain; 4 = Favourable; 5 = The least favourable).

Degree of Freedom: 3	Chi-Square (x^2): 5.32	$p<0.25$

Table 4.13: Customers' Perception of Hypermarket Offering the Best Service

Scale / Nationality	Carrefour 1	LuLu 2	Carrefour and LuLu 3	Other 4	Total	Mode	Mean	Median	SD
Omani N	101	280	36	14	431	2	1.91	2	0.66
%	23.43	64.97	8.35	3.25	100				
Non-Omani N	91	288	24	4	407	2	1.86	2	0.55
%	22.36	70.76	5.9	0.98	100				
Total N	192	568	60	18	838	2	1.89	2	0.61
%	22.91	67.78	7.16	2.15	100				

Degree of Freedom: 3	Chi-Square (x^2) 7.91	$p<0.050$

Table 4.14: Customers' Perception of Hypermarket Having the Best Products

Scale / Nationality	Carrefour 1	LuLu 2	Carrefour and LuLu 3	Other 4	Total	Mode	Mean	Median	SD
Omani N	92	299	24	16	431	2	1.92	2	0.642
%	21.35	69.37	5.57	3.71	100				
Non-Omani N	89	279	32	7	407	2	1.89	2	0.596
%	21.87	68.55	7.86	1.72	100				
Total N	181	578	56	23	838	2	1.91	2	0.620
%	21.6	68.97	6.68	2.74	100				

Degree of Freedom: 3	Chi-Square (x^2): 4.72	$p<0.25$ (0.193)

Table 4.15: Customers' Perception of Hypermarkets' Having Special Products (e.g., from countries of origin & delicatessen)

Scale / Nationality	Carrefour 1	LuLu 2	Carrefour and LuLu 3	Other 4	Total	Mode	Mean	Median	SD
Omani N	99	312	18	2	431	2	1.82	2	0.51
%	22.97	72.39	4.18	0.46	100				
Non-Omani N	74	273	39	21	407	2	2.02	2	0.70
%	18.18	67.08	9.58	5.16	100				
Total N	173	585	57	23	838	2	1.92	2	0.61
%	20.64	69.81	6.8	2.74	100				

Degree of Freedom: 3	Chi-Square (x^2): 28.98	$p<0.01$

Table 4.16: Customers' Perception of Hypermarket Offering the Best Raffles and Prizes

Scale / Nationality	Carrefour 1	LuLu 2	Carrefour and LuLu 3	Other 4	Total	Mode	Mean	Median	SD
Omani N	31	383	12	5	431	2	1.98	2	0.38
%	7.19	88.86	2.78	1.16	100				
Non-Omani N	29	301	39	38	407	2	2.21	2	0.71
%	7.13	73.96	9.58	9.34	100				
Total N	60	684	51	43	838	2	2.09	2	0.57
%	7.16	81.62	6.09	5.13	100				

Degree of Freedom: 3	Chi-Square (x^2): 48.87	$p<0.01$

Table 4.17: Customers' Frequency of Using Carrefour's Services

Scale Nationality	Always 1	Often 2	Sometimes 3	Never 4	Total	Mode	Mean	Median	SD
Omani N	3	12	37	3	55	3	2.73	3	0.65
%	5.45	21.82	67.27	5.45	100				
Non-Omani N	8	9	40	6	63	3	2.70	3	0.82
%	12.7	14.29	63.49	9.52	100				
Total N	11	21	77	9	118	3	2.71	3	0.74
%	9.32	17.8	65.25	7.63	100				

Degree of Freedom: 3	Chi-Square (x^2): 3.29	$p<0.5$ (0.349)

Table 4.18: Customers' Perception of the Availability of Carrefour's Services

Scale Nationality	Always 1	Often 2	Sometimes 3	Never 4	Total	Mode	Mean	Median	SD
Omani N	4	11	11	29	55	4	3.18	4	1.00
%	7.27	20	20	52.73	100				
Non-Omani N	6	7	44	6	63	3	2.79	3	0.74
%	9.52	11.11	69.84	9.52	100				
Total N	10	18	55	35	118	3	2.97	3	0.89
%	8.47	15.25	46.61	29.66	100				

Degree of Freedom: 3	Chi-Square (x^2): 35.83	$p<0.01$

Table 4.19: Customers' Perception of Getting the Expected Service in Carrefour

Scale Nationality	Always 1	Often 2	Sometimes 3	Never 4	Total	Mode	Mean	Median	SD
Omani N	2	3	21	29	55	3	3.40	4	0.76
%	3.64	5.45	38.18	52.73	100				
Non-Omani N	4	11	38	10	63	3	2.86	3	0.76
%	6.35	17.46	60.32	15.87	100				
Total N	6	14	59	39	118	3	3.11	3	0.80
%	5.08	11.86	50.00%	33.05	100				

Degree of Freedom: **3**	Chi-Square (x^2): **18.94**	$p<0.01$

Table 4.20: Customers' Perception of Having Their Complaints Taken Seriously in Carrefour

Scale Nationality	Always 1	Often 2	Sometimes 3	Never 4	Total	Mode	Mean	Median	SD
Omani N	37	3	12	3	55	1	1.65	1	1.00
%	67.27	5.45	21.82	5.45	100				
Non-Omani N	7	10	34	12	63	3	2.81	3	0.88
%	11.11	15.87	53.97	19.05	100				
Total N	44	13	46	15	118	3	2.27	3	1.10
%	37.29	11.02	38.98	12.71	100				

Degree of Freedom: **3**	Chi-Square (x^2): **39.79**	$p<0.01$

**Table 4.21: Customers' Perception of Receiving Satisfactory Solutions
or Help in Carrefour**

Scale Nationality	Always 1	Often 2	Sometimes 3	Never 4	Total	Mode	Mean	Median	SD
Omani N	4	29	17	5	55	2	2.42	2	0.76
%	7.27	52.73	30.91	9.09	100				
Non-Omani N	10	12	32	9	63	3	2.63	3	0.92
%	15.87	19.05	50.79	14.29	100				
Total N	14	41	49	14	118	3	2.53	3	0.85
%	11.86	34.75	41.53	11.86	100				

Degree of Freedom: **3**	Chi-Square (x^2): 14.88	$p<0.01$

Table 4.22: Customers' Frequency of Using LuLu's Services

Scale Nationality	Always 1	Often 2	Sometimes 3	Never 4	Total	Mode	Mean	Median	SD
Omani N	9	9	290	10	318	3	2.95	3	0.41
%	2.83	2.83	91.19	3.14	100				
Non-Omani N	30	230	8	4	272	2	1.95	2	0.44
%	11.03	84.56	2.94	1.47	100				
Total N	39	239	298	14	590	3	2.49	3	0.66
%	6.61	40.51	50.51	2.37	100				

Degree of Freedom: **3**	Chi-Square (x^2): 484.45	$p<0.01$

Table 4.23: Customers' Perception of the Availability of LuLu's Services

Scale / Nationality	Always 1	Often 2	Sometimes 3	Never 4	Total	Mode	Mean	Median	SD
Omani N	30	270	6	12	318	2	2.00	2	0.51
%	9.43	84.91	1.89	3.77	100				
Non-Omani N	32	228	7	5	272	2	1.94	2	0.46
%	11.76	83.82	2.57	1.84	100				
Total N	62	498	13	17	590	2	1.97	2	0.49
%	10.51	84.41	2.2	2.88	100				

Degree of Freedom: **3**	Chi-Square (x^2): 3.00	$p<0.5$ (0.392)

Table 4.24: Customers' Perception of Getting the Expected Service in LuLu

Scale / Nationality	Always 1	Often 2	Sometimes 3	Never 4	Total	Mode	Mean	Median	SD
Omani N	66	245	5	2	318	2	1.82	2	0.47
%	20.75	77.04	1.57	0.63	100				
Non-Omani N	29	240	2	1	272	2	1.91	2	0.35
%	10.66	88.24	0.74	0.37	100				
Total N	95	485	7	3	590	2	1.86	2	0.42
%	16.1	82.2	1.19	0.51	100				

Degree of Freedom: **3**	Chi-Square (x^2): 12.57	$p<0.01$

Table 4.25: Customers' Perception of Having Their Complaints Taken Seriously in LuLu

Scale / Nationality	Always 1	Often 2	Sometimes 3	Never 4	Total	Mode	Mean	Median	SD
Omani N	29	269	16	4	318	2	1.98	2	0.44
%	9.12	84.59	5.03	1.26	100				
Non-Omani N	222	40	8	2	272	1	1.23	1	0.53
%	81.62	14.71	2.94	0.74	100				
Total N	251	309	24	6	590	2	1.64	2	0.61
%	42.54	52.37	4.07	1.02	100				

Degree of Freedom: 3	Chi-Square (x^2): 319.81	$p < 0.01$

Table 4.26: Customers' Perception of Receiving Satisfactory Solutions or Help in LuLu

Scale / Nationality	Always 1	Often 2	Sometimes 3	Never 4	Total	Mode	Mean	Median	SD
Omani N	220	80	14	4	318	2	1.38	1	0.63
%	69.18	25.16	4.4	1.26	100				
Non-Omani N	231	27	12	2	272	1	1.21	1	0.55
%	84.93	9.93	4.41	0.74	100				
Total N	451	107	26	6	590	1	1.3	1	0.60
%	76.44	18.14	4.41	1.02	100				

Degree of Freedom: 3	Chi-Square (x^2): 23.90	$p < 0.01$

**Table 4.27: Customers' Frequency of Using Other Supermarkets'/
Hypermarkets' Services**

Scale / Nationality	Always 1	Often 2	Sometimes 3	Never 4	Total	Mode	Mean	Median	SD
Omani N	2	47	7	2	58	2	2.16	2	0.52
%	3.45	81.03	12.07	3.45	100				
Non-Omani N	4	36	27	5	72	2	2.46	2	0.71
%	5.56	50.00	37.5	6.94	100				
Total N	6	83	34	7	130	2	2.32	2	0.65
%	4.62	63.85	26.15	5.38	100				

Degree of Freedom: 3	Chi-Square (x^2): 13.83	$p < 0.01$

**Table 4.28: Customers' Perception of the Availability of Other
Supermarkets'/Hypermarkets' Services**

Scale / Nationality	Always 1	Often 2	Sometimes 3	Never 4	Total	Mode	Mean	Median	SD
Omani N	4	42	10	2	58	2	2.17	2	0.60
%	6.9	72.41	17.24	3.45	100				
Non-Omani N	5	32	31	4	72	2	2.47	2	0.71
%	6.94	44.44	43.06	5.56	100				
Total N	9	74	41	6	130	2	2.34	2	0.68
%	6.92	56.92	31.54	4.62	100				

Degree of Freedom: 3	Chi-Square (x^2): 11.51	$p < 0.01$

Table 4.29: Customers' Perception of Getting the Expected Service in Other Supermarkets/Hypermarkets

Scale / Nationality	Always 1	Often 2	Sometimes 3	Never 4	Total	Mode	Mean	Median	SD
Omani N	20	32	6	0	58	2	1.76	2	0.63
%	34.48	55.17	10.34	0	100				
Non-Omani N	4	28	35	5	72	3	2.57	3	0.71
%	5.56	38.89	48.61	6.94	100				
Total N	24	60	41	5	130	2	2.21	2	0.78
%	18.46	46.15	31.54	3.85	100				

Degree of Freedom: 3	Chi-Square (x^2): 35.35	$p<0.01$

Table 4.30: Customers' Perception of Having Their Complaints Taken Seriously in Other Supermarkets/Hypermarkets

Scale / Nationality	Always 1	Often 2	Sometimes 3	Never 4	Total	Mode	Mean	Median	SD
Omani N	22	28	4	4	58	2	1.83	2	0.84
%	37.93	48.28	6.9	6.9	100				
Non-Omani N	4	30	33	5	72	3	2.54	3	0.71
%	5.56	41.67	45.83	6.94	100				
Total N	26	58	37	9	130	2	2.22	2	0.85
%	20	44.62	28.46	6.92	100				

Degree of Freedom: 3	Chi-Square (x^2): 34.26	$p<0.01$

Table 4.31: Customers' Perception of Receiving Satisfactory Solutions or Help in Other Supermarkets/Hypermarkets

Scale	Always	Often	Sometimes	Never	Total	Mode	Mean	Median	SD
Nationality	1	2	3	4					
Omani N	4	42	6	6	58	2	2.241	2	0.733
%	6.9	72.41	10.34	10.34	100				
Non-Omani N	6	32	30	4	72	2	2.44	2	0.729
%	8.33	44.44	41.67	5.56	100				
Total N	10	74	36	10	130	2	2.354	2	0.735
%	7.69	56.92	27.69	7.69	100				

Degree of Freedom: 3	Chi-Square (x^2): 16.84	$p<0.01$

Appendix F

Tables 5.1- 5.20

Table 5.1: Staff's *Perception* of the Actual Situation – Job Description

Scale/ Hypermarket	Strongly Disagree 5	Neutral 3	Disagree 4	Agree 2	Strongly Agree 1	Total	Mode	Median	Mean	SD
Carrefour N	1	10	40	1	1	53	4	4	3.74	0.62
%	1.89	18.87	75.47	1.89	1.89	100.00				
LuLu N	1	9	1	46	3	60	2	2	2.18	0.62
%	1.67	15.00	1.67	76.67	5.00	100.00				
Total N	2	19	41	47	4	113	2	3	2.91	1.00
Total %	1.77	16.81	36.28	41.59	3.54	100.00				

Pearson Chi^2(x^2): 81.11	Degrees of freedom: 4	$p<0.001$
Two tailed t-test: 13.19	Degrees of freedom: 111	$p<0.001$

Table 5.2: Staff's *Satisfaction* with the Actual Situation – Job Description

Scale/ Hypermarket	Strongly Disagree 5	Neutral 3	Disagree 4	Agree 2	Strongly Agree 1	Total	Mode	Median	Mean	SD
Carrefour N	2	30	19	1	1	53	4	4	3.58	0.69
%	3.77	56.60	35.85	1.89	1.89	100.00				
LuLu N	2	3	8	42	5	60	2	2	2.25	0.82
%	3.33	5.00	13.33	70.00	8.33	100.00				
Total N	4	33	27	43	6	113	2	3	2.88	1.01
Total %	1.77	36.28	16.81	41.59	3.54	100.00				

Pearson Chi^2(x^2): 68.16	Degrees of freedom: 4	$p<0.001$
Two tailed t-test: 9.32	Degrees of freedom: 111	$p<0.001$

Table 5.3: Staff's *Perception* of the Actual Situation –
Having Clear Rules

Scale/ Hypermarket	Strongly Disagree 5	Disagree 4	Neutral 3	Agree 2	Strongly Agree 1	Total	Mode	Median	Mean	SD
Carrefour N	2	39	9	2	1	53	4	4	3.74	0.68
%	3.77	73.58	16.98	3.77	1.89	100.00				
LuLu N	1	2	7	47	3	60	2	2	2.18	0.65
%	1.67	3.33	11.67	78.33	5.00	100.00				
Total N	3	41	16	49	4	113	2	3	2.91	1.02
Total %	2.65	36.28	14.16	43.36	3.54	100.00				

Pearson Chi^2(x^2): 76.16	Degrees of freedom:4	$p<0.001$
Two tailed *t*-test: 12.36	Degrees of freedom: 111	$p<0.001$

Table 5.4: Staff's *Satisfaction* with the Actual Situation –
Having Clear Rules

Scale/ Hypermarket	Strongly Disagree 5	Disagree 4	Neutral 3	Agree 2	Strongly Agree 1	Total	Mode	Median	Mean	SD
Carrefour N	5	38	7	2	1	53	4	4	3.83	0.73
%	9.43	71.70	13.21	3.77	1.89	100.00				
LuLu N	2	3	7	40	8	60	2	2	2.18	0.85
%	3.33	5.00	11.67	66.67	13.33	100.00				
Total N	7	41	14	42	9	113	2	3	2.96	1.14
Total %	6.19	36.28	12.39	37.17	7.96	100.00				

Pearson Chi^2(x^2): 70.83	Degrees of freedom:4	$p<0.001$
Two tailed *t*-test: 10.97	Degrees of freedom: 111	$p<0.001$

Table 5.5: Staff's *Perception* of the Actual Situation – Having to write Daily Reports

Scale/ Hypermarket	Strongly Disagree 5	Disagree 4	Neutral 3	Agree 2	Strongly Agree 1	Total	Mode	Median	Mean	SD
Carrefour N	45	4	2	1	1	53	5	5	4.72	0.79
%	84.91	7.55	3.77	1.89	1.89	100.00				
LuLu N	1	45	9	3	2	60	4	4	3.67	0.75
%	1.67	75.00	15.00	5.00	3.33	100.00				
Total N	46	49	11	4	3	113	4	4	4.16	0.93
Total %	40.71	43.36	9.73	3.54	2.65	100.00				

Pearson Chi^2(x^2): 82.06	Degrees of freedom: 4	$p<0.001$
Two tailed *t*-test: 7.22	Degrees of freedom: 111	$p<0.001$

Table 5.6: Staff's *Satisfaction* with the Actual Situation – Having to Write Daily Reports

Scale/ Hypermarket	Strongly Disagree 5	Neutral 3	Disagree 4	Agree 2	Strongly Agree 1	Total	Mode	Median	Mean	SD
Carrefour N	1	40	10	1	1	53.00	4	4	3.749	0.625
%	1.89	75.47	18.87	1.89	1.89	100.00				
LuLu N	2	2	6	45	5	60	2	2	2.18	0.77
%	3.33	3.33	10.00	75.00	8.33	100.00				
Total N	3	42	16	46	6	113	2	3	2.91	1.05
Total %	2.65	37.17	14.16	40.71	5.31	100.00				

Pearson Chi^2(x^2): 80.34	Degrees of freedom: 4	$p<0.001$
Two tailed *t*-test: 11.67	Degrees of freedom: 111	$p<0.001$

Table 5.7: Staff's *Perception* of the Actual Situation – Communication through Formal Channels

Scale/ Hypermarket	Strongly Disagree 5	Disagree 4	Neutral 3	Agree 2	Strongly Agree 1	Total	Mode	Median	Mean	SD
Carrefour N	5	5	41	1	1	53	3	3	3.23	0.72
%	9.43	9.43	77.36	1.89	1.89	100.00				
LuLu N	1	2	53	2	2	60	3	3	2.97	0.52
%	1.67	3.33	88.33	3.33	3.33	100.00				
Total N	6	7	94	3	3	113	3	3	3.09	0.63
Total %	5.31	6.19	83.19	2.65	2.65	100.00				

Pearson Chi²(x^2): 5.74	Degrees of freedom: 4	$p < 0.25$
Two tailed t-test: 2.21	Degrees of freedom: 111	$p < 0.05$

Table 5.8: Staff's *Satisfaction* with the Actual Situation – Communication through Formal Channels

Scale/ Hypermarket	Strongly Disagree 5	Disagree 4	Neutral 3	Agree 2	Strongly Agree 1	Total	Mode	Median	Mean	SD
Carrefour N	2	33	14	2	2	53	4	4	3.58	0.80
%	3.77	62.26	26.42	3.77	3.77	100.00				
LuLu N	3	3	7	42	5	60	2	2	2.28	0.88
%	5.00	5.00	11.67	70.00	8.33	100.00				
Total N	5	36	21	44	7	113	2	3	2.89	1.06
Total %	4.42	31.86	18.58	38.94	6.19	100.00				

Pearson Chi²(x^2): 65.00	Degrees of freedom: 4	$p < 0.001$
Two tailed t-test: 8.18	Degrees of freedom: 111	$p < 0.001$

Table 5.9: Staff's *Perception* of the Actual Situation – Having Say in Decisions

Scale/ Hypermarket	Strongly Disagree 5	Disagree 4	Neutral 3	Agree 2	Strongly Agree 1	Total	Mode	Median	Mean	SD
Carrefour N	4	45	2	1	1	53.00	4	4	3.95	0.60
%	7.55	84.91	3.77	1.89	1.89	100.00				
LuLu N	2	2	6	45	5	60.00	2	2	2.18	0.77
%	3.33	3.33	10.00	75.00	8.33	100.00				
Total N	6	47	8	46	6	113.00	4	3	3.01	1.12
Total %	5.31	41.59	7.08	40.71	5.31	100.00				

Pearson Chi^2(x^2): 86.66	Degrees of freedom: 4	$p<0.001$
Two tailed *t*-test: 13.41	Degrees of freedom: 111	$p<0.001$

Table 5.10: Staff's *Satisfaction* with the Actual Situation – Having Say in Decisions

Scale/ Hypermarket	Strongly Disagree 5	Disagree 4	Neutral 3	Agree 2	Strongly Agree 1	Total	Mode	Median	Mean	SD
Carrefour N	1	45	4	2	1	53	4	4	3.81	0.62
%	1.89	84.91	7.55	3.77	1.89	100.00				
LuLu N	2	2	10	38	8	60	2	2	2.2	0.84
%	3.33	3.33	16.67	63.33	13.33	100.00				
Total N	3	47	14	40	9	113	4	3	2.96	1.10
Total %	2.65	41.59	12.39	35.4	7.96	100.00				

Pearson Chi^2(x^2): 79.96	Degrees of freedom: 4	$p<0.001$
Two tailed *t*-test: 11.46	Degrees of freedom: 111	$p<0.001$

Table 5.11: Staff's *Perception* of the Actual Situation –Freedom to Communicate Upwards and Downwards

Scale/ Hypermarket	Strongly Disagree 5	Disagree 4	Neutral 3	Agree 2	Strongly Agree 1	Total	Mode	Median	Mean	SD
Carrefour N	2	39	10	1	1	53	4	4	3.75	0.65
%	3.77	73.58	18.87	1.89	1.89	100.00				
LuLu N	2	13	5	38	2	60	2	2	2.58	0.98
%	3.33	21.67	8.33	63.33	3.33	100.00				
Total N	4	52	15	39	3	113	4	3	3.13	1.02
Total %	3.54	46.02	13.27	34.51	2.65	100.00				

Pearson Chi^2 (x^2): 49.86	Degrees of freedom: 4	$p<0.001$
Two tailed *t*-test: 7.39	Degrees of freedom: 111	$p<0.001$

Table 5.12: Staff's *Satisfaction* with the Actual Situation Freedom to Communicate Upwards and Downwards

Scale/ Hypermarket	Strongly Disagree 5	Disagree 4	Neutral 3	Agree 2	Strongly Agree 1	Total	Mode	Median	Mean	SD
Carrefour N	3	39	7	3	1	53	4	4	3.75	0.73
%	5.66	73.58	13.21	5.66	1.89	100.00				
LuLu N	2	6	7	41	4	60	2	2	2.35	0.88
%	3.33	10.00	11.67	68.33	6.67	100.00				
Total N	5	45	14	44	5	113	4	3	3.01	1.07
Total %	4.42	39.82	12.39	38.94	4.42	100.00				

Pearson Chi^2 (x^2): 58.81	Degrees of freedom: 4	$p<0.001$
Two tailed *t*-test: 9.16	Degrees of freedom: 111	$p<0.001$

Table 5.13: Staff's *Perception* of the Actual Situation – Access to Data and Information

Scale/ Hypermarket	Strongly Disagree 5	Disagree 4	Neutral 3	Agree 2	Strongly Agree 1	Total	Mode	Median	Mean	SD
Carrefour N	1	40	10	1	1	53	4	4	3.74	0.62
%	1.89	75.47	18.87	1.89	1.89	100.00				
LuLu N	1	2	7	45	5	60	2	2	2.15	0.68
%	1.67	3.33	11.67	75.00	8.33	100.00				
Total N	2	42	17	46	6	113	2	3	2.89	1.03
Total %	1.77	37.17	15.04	40.71	5.31	100.00				

Pearson Chi^2(x^2): 79.54	Degrees of freedom: 4	$p<0.001$
Two tailed *t*-test: 12.80	Degrees of freedom: 111	$p<0.001$

Table 5.14: Staff's *Satisfaction* with the Actual Situation – Access to Data and Information

Scale/ Hypermarket	Strongly Disagree 5	Disagree 4	Neutral 3	Agree 2	Strongly Agree 1	Total	Mode	Median	Mean	SD
Carrefour N	1	40	8	3	1	53	4	4	3.70	0.70
%	1.89	75.47	15.09	5.66	1.89	100.00				
LuLu N	1	2	8	45	4	60	2	2	2.18	0.68
%	1.67	3.33	13.33	75.00	6.67	100.00				
Total N	2	42	16	48	5	113	2	3	2.89	1.02
Total %	1.77	37.17	14.16	42.48	4.42	100.00				

Pearson Chi^2(x^2): 72.78	Degrees of freedom: 4	$p<0.001$
Two tailed *t*-test: 11.72	Degrees of freedom: 111	$p<0.001$

Table 5.15: Staff's *Perception* of the Actual Situation – Giving Feedback and ability to Criticize Superiors

Scale/	Strongly Disagree	Disagree	Neutral	Agree	Strongly Agree	Total	Mode	Median	Mean	SD
Hypermarket	5	4	3	2	1					
Carrefour N	2	43	5	1	2	53	4	4	3.79	0.72
%	3.77	81.13	9.43	1.89	3.77	100.00				
LuLu N	10	38	5	2	5	60	4	4	3.77	1.05
%	16.67	63.33	8.33	3.33	8.33	100.00				
Total N	12	81	10	3	7	113	4	4	3.78	0.90
Total %	10.62	71.68	8.85	2.65	6.19	100.00				

Pearson Chi^2 (x^2): 6.85	Degrees of freedom: 4	$p<0.25$
Two tailed t-test: 0.15	Degrees of freedom: 111	$p>0.20$

Table 5.16: Staff's *Satisfaction* with the Actual Situation - Giving Feedback and ability to Criticise Superiors

Scale/	Strongly Disagree	Disagree	Neutral	Agree	Strongly Agree	Total	Mode	Median	Mean	SD
Hypermarket	5	4	3	2	1					
Carrefour N	5	37	9	1	1	53	4	4	3.83	0.70
%	9.43	69.81	16.98	1.89	1.89	100.00				
LuLu N	2	40	10	6	2	60	4	4	3.57	0.85
%	3.33	66.67	16.67	10.00	3.33	100.00				
Total N	7	77	19	7	3	113	4	4	3.69	0.79
Total %	6.19	68.14	16.81	6.19	2.65	100.00				

Pearson Chi^2 (x^2): 4.95	Degrees of freedom: 4	$p<0.5$
Two tailed t-test: 1.78	Degrees of freedom: 111	$p<0.1$

Table 5.17: Staff's Attitude in Presenting Their Company as a Great Place to Work in

Scale/ Hypermarket	Strongly Disagree 5	Disagree 4	Neutral 3	Agree 2	Strongly Agree 1	Total	Mode	Median	Mean	SD
Carrefour N	4	4	42	2	1	53.00	3	3	3.15	0.69
%	7.55	7.55	79.25	3.77	1.89	100.00				
LuLu N	1	2	5	45	7	60	2	2	2.08	0.70
%	1.67	3.33	8.33	75.00	11.67	100.00				
Total N	5	6	47	47	8	113	2 & 3	3	2.58	0.87
Total %	4.42	5.31	41.59	41.59	7.08	100.00				

Pearson Chi²(x²): 75.29	Degrees of freedom: 4	$p < 0.001$
Two tailed t-test: 8.17	Degrees of freedom: 111	$p < 0.001$

Table 5.18: Staff's Attitude - Having Pride in Their Company

Scale/ Hypermarket	Strongly Disagree 5	Disagree 4	Neutral 3	Agree 2	Strongly Agree 1	Total	Mode	Median	Mean	SD
Carrefour N	1	2	6	40	4	53	2	2	2.17	0.70
%	1.89	3.77	11.32	75.47	7.55	100.00				
LuLu N	2	3	5	45	5	60	2	2	2.20	0.80
%	3.33	5.00	8.33	75.00	8.33	100.00				
Total N	3	5	11	85	9	113	2	2	2.19	0.75
Total %	2.65	4.42	9.73	75.22	7.96	100.00				

Pearson Chi²(x²): 0.60	Degrees of freedom: 4	$p < 0.995$
Two tailed t-test: -0.21	Degrees of freedom: 111	$p > 0.20$

Table 5.19: Staff's Attitude - Company Provides Inspiration

Scale/ Hypermarket	Strongly Disagree 5	Disagree 4	Neutral 3	Agree 2	Strongly Agree 1	Total	Mode	Median	Mean	SD
Carrefour N	2	40	8	2	1	53	4	4	3.75	0.68
%	3.77	75.47	15.09	3.77	1.89	100.00				
LuLu N	1	2	6	47	4	60	2	2	2.15	0.66
%	1.67	3.33	10.00	78.33	6.67	100.00				
Total N	3	42	14	49	5	113	2	3	2.90	1.04
Total %	2.65	37.17	12.39	43.36	4.42	100.00				

Pearson Chi^2(x^2): 78.00	Degrees of freedom: 4	$p<0.001$
Two tailed t-test: 12.75	Degrees of freedom: 111	$p<0.001$

Table 5.20: Staff's Attitude - Caring about the Interest of Company

Scale/ Hypermarket	Strongly Disagree 5	Disagree 4	Neutral 3	Agree 2	Strongly Agree 1	Total	Mode	Median	Mean	SD
Carrefour N	1	18	30	2	2	53	3	3	3.26	0.74
%	1.89	33.96	56.6	3.77	3.77	100.00				
LuLu N	2	3	5	45	5	60	2	2	2.20	0.80
%	3.33	5.00	8.33	75.00	8.33	100.00				
Total N	3	21	35	47	7	113	2	3	2.70	0.93
Total %	2.65	18.58	30.97	41.59	6.19	100.00				

Pearson Chi^2(x^2): 69.36	Degrees of freedom: 4	$p<0.001$
Two tailed t-test: 7.33	Degrees of freedom: 111	$p<0.001$

www.ingramcontent.com/pod-product-compliance
Lightning Source LLC
Chambersburg PA
CBHW081127170526
45165CB00008B/2574